RiCE

RiCE

from risotto to rice pudding

MURDOCH
BOOKS

contents

the grain of life

In so many countries, rice is 'the grain of life'. It has shaped not only the diet, but also the culture and commerce, of billions of people around the world. High in carbohydrate, iron and protein, this unassuming little cereal grain is a powerhouse of nutrition.

There are more than 2000 types of rice. You will find a good selection at the supermarket, sold under its culinary use (pudding rice), according to its method of processing (precooked), place of origin (Valencia) or its degree of stickiness (glutinous). But mostly, rice is classified by the shape, or size, of the grain.

Long grain is long and slender. The grains usually stay separate and fluffy after cooking, so this is the best choice if you want to serve it as a side dish, or as a bed for sauces. Medium-grain rice is shorter and plumper, and the most absorbent types work well in paella and risotto. Short-grain rice is almost round, with moist grains that stick together. It's perfect for rice pudding. Then there are the speciality grains, such as red Camargue, black and purple rice, and wild rice (which is not a true rice but the seed of an American grass).

To show off the virtues of each variety, we've divided our recipes into three sections: long-grain; short-grain (medium-grain falls into both categories, depending on whether it is medium-long or medium-short); and coloured rice. In each chapter you'll find an array of delicious dishes from the world's greatest rice cuisines.

all about rice

selection

Supermarkets today stock a good range of rice, but if you frequent Asian food stores and speciality European food suppliers, you'll find an even wider variety of rice, each with its own special quality. To help you in your selection, before you buy rice, have some idea of how you want to prepare it. That way, you won't be forced to use a poor substitute in a recipe.

super species

Different types of rice have different cooking characteristics. The size of the grain is not the only distinction. Cultivated rice is further divided into two subspecies: the tropical *indica* rice which is long grained and nonsticky, like basmati; and *japonica* rice, a shorter grain with varying degrees of stickiness, grown in temperate climates, including Japanese, Spanish and Italian rice. Added to these is a third subspecies, *javanica*, also known as *bulu*— a tropical to subtropical, medium- to long-grain rice that is somewhat sticky.

the three senses

Texture, fragrance and colour are other ways of distinguishing rice. Sticky-textured rices (also known as glutinous or waxy) absorb less water during cooking and, once cooked, the grains lose their shape and stick together. This makes sticky rice suitable for sushi, puddings or any dish eaten with chopsticks. Although its name suggests otherwise, sticky rice contains no gluten. It comes as white or black rice and generally is a type of *japonica*, with Thai jasmine rice being an exception.

Aromatic rices have a distinctive taste and fragrance, and are delicious served plain with savoury dishes on the side. The most popular ones are jasmine—a soft, slightly clingy rice when cooked; basmati, which cooks into long, slender grains that are dry, separate and fluffy; and American Della, a drier, fluffier rice when cooked.

For an aesthetic effect, take a look at black or purple rice, red rice and wild rice. These are perfect for stuffings and salads, as an accompaniment to strong-flavoured dishes, or for puddings and other desserts.

mod-con rices

To accommodate busy lifestyles, innovative processing methods have been used to develop precooked (instant) rice—basically white rice that has been precooked and dehydrated so it cooks quickly. Its obvious advantage is convenience, but it is usually more expensive and lacks flavour.

A compromise between nutritious brown rice and tender, fast-cooking white rice is parboiled (converted) rice. The process was discovered in ancient India where it was used to preserve rice and retain the nutrients that are destroyed in milling. Because it is milled, parboiled rice has better storage qualities as it has no bran or germ oil to go rancid. Not all cooking methods are recommended for parboiled rice as it does not absorb water so easily. It is less suitable for dishes where flavour absorption is important, such as risotto or paella. The cooked grains of parboiled rice tend to have a slightly bouncy texture and are nonsticky.

storage

Once you have opened a fresh packet of rice, store it in a cool, dry place in an airtight container. Rice bought in large sacks is best stored in a dry, clean container with a lid. An unopened packet will keep for up to one year. Brown rice still contains the oil-rich germ or bran layer, so it will turn rancid if left in a warm place for too long, just like wholemeal flour. For this reason, it is best stored in an airtight container in the fridge. You also need to take extra care with cooked rice. If it is not consumed immediately, cover it, then chill it quickly as harmful bacteria can grow rapidly. Cooked rice will store in the fridge for up to two days.

cooking tips

Packaged rice does not require prior rinsing, but rice bought in sacks needs to be washed to remove dust and stones.

For well-cooked rice, it is important to get the rice-to-water ratio right. As a guide, in a saucepan, cover the rice with liquid to a depth of one finger joint above the rice. Then, use one of the following techniques.

Absorption method This is an efficient and nutritious way to cook rice, as nutrients are not discarded with the cooking water. Generally, long-grain rices suit this method. To cook, bring the water and rice to the boil, cover, then reduce the heat to a simmer. The rice is cooked by the hot water and by the remaining steam once the water has been absorbed. Simply fluff up with a fork and serve immediately.

Rapid boiling Like pasta, many rices, from arborio to parboiled rice, cook well in plenty of water. Bring a large saucepan of water to the boil, uncovered. Sprinkle in the rice and keep an eye on it, so it does not stick or overcook. Drain the rice in a sieve (if you are using jasmine or Japanese rice, rinse it with a little tepid water to prevent it cooking further).

Steaming rice This method is preferred for sticky rice. Soak the rice overnight, then drain. Spread out the grains in a steamer and put the steamer over a wok or pan of boiling water. The rice does not touch the water—it is cooked only by the steam.

long-grain rice

quick guide to long grains

Rice contains two types of starch in varying proportions—amylose and amylopectin. Long-grain rice has more amylose, which is harder to dissolve. This means that, generally, long-grain rice should be used when you want a dry, fluffy texture in your dish, with every grain separate. It's as perfect for the more complicated pilaffs of the Middle East and India as it is for a simple white rice side dish. Medium-to-long grains contain less amylose than long grains which makes them more suitable for stuffings and American-Creole rice dishes.

scented strains

Rice contains a compound that gives it a distinct fragrance and flavour, but aromatic rices (which tend to be long grain) have this substance in higher concentrations. When the rice is served hot, it is still aromatic.

There are some wonderfully fragrant rices from around the world that are well worth seeking out. Jasmine rice is a long grain produced in Thailand. It is named after the sweet-smelling jasmine flower of Southeast Asia because, on cooking, it releases a similar floral aroma (it is not related to the jasmine plant). Jasmine rice cooks to a soft, slightly clingy grain and its taste enhances the traditional spices of Thai dishes (see the recipe for stuffed mussels on page 61). It is also served plain as it requires no seasoning.

Basmati rice, another fragrant strain, grows in the Himalayan foothills in northern India and Pakistan. It cooks to a drier, firmer texture and the grains elongate on cooking. Other basmatis, from West Bengal, are labelled 'Patna'. These are ideal rices for Middle Eastern pilaffs, and north Indian pulaos and biryani.

hybrid grains

In the United States, American long-grain rice has been crossed with basmati to make the dry, fluffy Della variety of rice called Louisiana popcorn. It has a buttery popcorn flavour, but is not as fragrant as basmati. Texmati is very similar.

a second serve

There is more than one dish in every saucepan of fluffy rice. If you don't use a heat-tamer when you cook this style of rice, you may get a crusty layer on the bottom of the pan. This is prized in many cultures—it even gets its own name, depending on which country you are in.

In Thailand, they let the crusty rice dry in the sun, cut it into circles, deep-fry the circles and use them as a pick-up for dips. So, do not scrape the crusty layer at the bottom of the saucepan into your fluffy rice. Instead, leave it in the saucepan (it must be ovenproof) and dry it for a few minutes in a 150°C (300°F/Gas 2) oven. Then, scrape out the rice, break it up, and deep-fry the clumps for a tasty snack.

smart-cookers

If you tend to cook up large quantities of rice, you might want to invest in an electric cooker. These gadgets work wonders for fluffy long-grain rice and Japanese medium-to-long grains. The electric rice cooker is designed to cook rice the absorption way. It automatically switches off when the grains are cooked, so the rice is then steam-dried. Usually, though, it is only the portion closer to the surface which is steamed—the rice at the bottom of the cooker is boiled. This is why the rice closer to the top tastes so much better. The rice can be kept warm in the cooker for a few hours without any loss of quality.

13

creamy clam soup

This dish marries the fresh, briny flavour of clams with the luxurious taste of cream, while the rice imparts good texture. The recipe makes a smooth soup but you could leave it chunky, if you prefer. Reserve a few clams in the shell to decorate each serving bowl.

1.8 kg (4 lb 8 oz) clams, in shells, cleaned
1 litre (4 cups) fish stock
3 tablespoons butter
1 onion, peeled and chopped
1 celery stalk, trimmed and chopped
1 large carrot, peeled and chopped
2 large leeks, trimmed and sliced
  into rings
1 bay leaf
85 g (3 oz) long-grain rice
185 ml (3/4 cup) cream
3 tablespoons finely chopped parsley

Serves 4

Tip the clams into a large saucepan with 250 ml (1 cup) water. Put it over high heat, bring the liquid to the boil, then reduce the heat to medium and add a tight-fitting lid. Cook for 7–10 minutes—the shells will open when the clams are cooked. Drain and set aside the clams, discarding any that have not opened. Reserve the cooking liquid. Add enough fish stock to the liquid to make 1 litre (4 cups).

Rinse the saucepan, then return to the heat with the butter. Once the butter has melted, add the onion, celery, carrot and leek. Cook over a medium heat, covered, for 10 minutes, stirring occasionally. Add the stock and bay leaf, bring to the boil, reduce the heat and simmer for a further 10 minutes. Add the rice, bring the mixture back to the boil, cover and cook on medium heat for 15–20 minutes, or until the rice and vegetables are tender.

Meanwhile, remove all but eight of the cooked clams from the shells. When ready, remove the soup from the heat and stir in the shelled clams. Remove the bay leaf and allow to cool for 10 minutes.

Purée the soup in batches in a blender (a food processor can be used but it will not achieve the same smooth consistency). Rinse the saucepan. Pass the soup through a sieve back into the saucepan.

Stir in the cream and season with salt and pepper. Gently reheat the soup. When it is hot, add some parsley, then serve, adding two clams in the shell to each bowl.

dolmades (stuffed vine leaves)

24 vine leaves in brine
200 g (1 cup) long- or medium-grain rice
1 onion, finely chopped
1 tablespoon olive oil
60 g (2¼ oz) pine nuts, toasted
2 tablespoons currants
2 tablespoons chopped dill
1 tablespoon finely chopped mint
1 tablespoon finely chopped
   flat-leaf (Italian) parsley
80 ml (⅓ cup) olive oil, extra
2 tablespoons lemon juice
500 ml (2 cups) chicken stock

Makes 24

Soak the vine leaves in cold water for
15 minutes, then remove and pat dry. Cut
off any stems. Reserve some leaves to line
the saucepan and discard any that have
holes. Meanwhile, soak the rice in boiling
water for 10 minutes to soften, then drain.

Put the rice, onion, olive oil, pine nuts,
currants, herbs, and salt and pepper in a
large mixing bowl. Mix well to combine.

Lay some leaves, vein-side-down, on a flat
surface. Put 1 tablespoon of filling in the
centre of each leaf, fold the stalk end over
the filling, then the left and right sides to the
centre, and finally roll firmly towards the
tip. Repeat with the remaining leaves.

Use the reserved leaves to line the base of
a large, heavy-based saucepan. Drizzle with
1 tablespoon of olive oil. Add the
dolmades, packing them tightly in one
layer, then pour over the remaining olive oil
and lemon juice.

Pour the stock over the dolmades and cover
with an inverted plate to stop the dolmades
moving around while cooking. Bring to
the boil, then reduce the heat and simmer,
covered, for 45 minutes. Remove the
dolmades with a slotted spoon. Serve warm
or cold with lemon wedges, if you like.

yoghurt rice

4 tablespoons chana dal (yellow
  Bengal gram)
200 g (1 cup) basmati rice
2 tablespoons oil
1/2 teaspoon white mustard seeds
12 curry leaves
3 dried chillies
1/4 teaspoon ground turmeric
pinch of asafoetida
500 g (2 cups) plain Greek-style yoghurt

Serves 4

Soak the chana dal in 250 ml (1 cup) of
boiling water for 3 hours. Put the rice in
a sieve and wash under cold running
water until the water runs clear. Drain.

Put the rice and 500 ml (2 cups) of water
in a saucepan, and bring rapidly to the
boil. Stir, cover, reduce the heat to a slow
simmer and cook for 10 minutes. Leave for
15 minutes before fluffing up with a fork.

Drain the dal and pat dry with paper
towels. Heat the oil in a small saucepan
over low heat, add the mustard seeds,
cover, then shake the pan until the seeds
start to pop. Add the curry leaves, dried
chillies and dal, and fry for 2 minutes,
stirring occasionally. Stir in the ground
turmeric and asafoetida.

Put the yoghurt in a large bowl, pour the
fried dal mixture into the yoghurt and
mix thoroughly. Add the rice to the spicy
yoghurt and mix well. Season with salt.
Cover and refrigerate. Serve cold, but
before serving, stand the rice at room
temperature for about 10 minutes. Serve
as part of a meal. Yoghurt rice goes well
with meat dishes.

prawn pulao

200 g (1 cup) basmati rice
300 g (10 1/2 oz) small prawns (shrimp)
3 tablespoons oil
1 onion, finely chopped
1 stick of cinnamon
6 cardamom pods
5 cloves
1 stalk lemon grass, finely chopped
4 garlic cloves, crushed
5 cm (2 in) piece of fresh ginger, grated
1/4 teaspoon ground turmeric

Serves 4

Wash the rice under cold running water
and drain. Peel and devein the prawns,
then wash and pat dry with paper towels.

Heat the oil in a frying pan over a low heat
and fry the onion, spices and lemon grass.
Stir in the garlic, ginger and turmeric. Add
the prawns and stir until pink. Toss in the
rice and fry for 2 minutes. Pour in 500 ml
(2 cups) of boiling water and add a pinch
of salt. Bring to the boil. Reduce the heat
and simmer for 15 minutes. Remove from
the heat, cover and stand for 10 minutes.
Fluff up the rice before serving.

lamb biryani

This is an Indian rice and lamb dish in which both ingredients are cooked together in a sealed container. Browning the lamb first isn't essential but makes for a tastier dish. For the best results, use a large cast iron or enamelled casserole with a tight-fitting lid.

1 kg (2 lb 4 oz) boneless lamb leg or shoulder, cut into 3 cm (1¼ in) cubes
7 cm (3 in) piece of fresh ginger, grated
2 garlic cloves, crushed
2 tablespoons garam masala
½ teaspoon chilli powder
½ teaspoon ground turmeric
4 green chillies, finely chopped
4 tablespoons chopped coriander (cilantro) leaves
4 tablespoons chopped mint leaves
500 g (2½ cups) basmati rice
4 onions, thinly sliced
¼ teaspoon salt
125 ml (½ cup) oil
125 g (4½ oz) unsalted butter
250 g (1 cup) plain Greek-style yoghurt
½ teaspoon saffron strands, soaked in 2 tablespoons hot milk
3 tablespoons lemon juice

sealing dough
200 g (7 oz) plain (all-purpose) flour
1 teaspoon salt

Serves 6

Mix the lamb with the ginger, garlic, garam masala, chilli powder, turmeric, chilli, coriander and mint. Cover and marinate in the fridge overnight.

Wash the rice in a sieve under cold, running water until the water runs clear. Put the onion in a sieve, sprinkle with the salt and leave for 10 minutes to drain off any liquid that oozes out. Rinse and pat dry. Heat the oil and butter in a large, heavy-based saucepan, add the onion and fry for 10 minutes. Drain through a sieve, reserving the oil and butter.

Remove the lamb from the marinade, reserving the marinade. Fry the lamb in batches in a little of the oil and butter until well browned. Transfer the lamb to a casserole and add the browned onion, any remaining marinade and the yoghurt. Cook over low heat for 30 minutes, or until the lamb is tender.

In a separate saucepan, boil enough water to cover the rice. Add the rice, return the water to the boil and cook the rice for 5 minutes, then drain. Spread the rice evenly over the meat. Pour 2 tablespoons of the leftover oil and butter over the rice and drizzle with the saffron and milk.

To make the sealing dough, preheat the oven to 220°C (425°F/Gas 7). Make a dough by mixing the flour and salt with a little water. Roll it into a sausage shape and use it to seal the lid onto the rim of the pot, pressing it along the rim. Put the pot over high heat for 5 minutes to bring the contents to the boil, then transfer it to the oven for 40 minutes. Remove the pot and break the seal of the dough.

red capsicums can be turned into capsules of flavour

stuffed capsicums

long-grain rice

stuffed capsicums

150 g (3/4 cup) long- or medium-grain rice
315 ml (1 1/4 cups) chicken stock
6 medium-sized red, yellow or orange
   capsicums (peppers)
60 g (2 1/4 oz) pine nuts
80 ml (1/3 cup) olive oil
1 onion, chopped
125 g (1/2 cup) tomato passata
60 g (2 1/4 oz) currants
2 1/2 tablespoons chopped
   flat-leaf (Italian) parsley
1/2 teaspoon ground cinnamon
2 1/2 tablespoons chopped fresh
   mint leaves

Serves 6

Put the rice and stock in a saucepan, and
bring to the boil over medium heat. Reduce
the heat to medium-low, cover and cook
for 15 minutes or until tender. Remove from
the heat and set aside, covered.

Bring a large saucepan of water to the boil.
Cut off the tops of the capsicum, reserving
the lids, remove the seeds and membrane,
and discard. Blanch the capsicum (not the
lids) in the boiling water for 2 minutes.
Drain and upturn on paper towels to dry.

Preheat the oven to 180°C (350°F/Gas 4).
Toast the pine nuts in a frying pan over low
heat until golden brown, remove from the
pan and set aside. Increase the heat to
medium and heat 2 tablespoons of oil. Add
the onion and cook for 10 minutes.

Add the passata, currants, cinnamon, herbs,
rice and pine nuts to the pan, and stir for
2 minutes. Season with salt and pepper.

Stand the capsicum in a baking dish so they
fit snugly. Divide the rice mixture between
the capsicum cavities. Replace the capsicum
lids. Pour 100 ml (3 1/2 fl oz) boiling water
into the dish and drizzle the remaining oil
over the tops of the capsicum. Bake for
40 minutes or until cooked through.

tomates yemistes
(rice-stuffed tomatoes)

8 medium-sized tomatoes
100 g (1/2 cup) long- or medium-grain rice
2 tablespoons olive oil
1 red onion, finely chopped
1 garlic clove, crushed
1 teaspoon dried oregano
40 g (1/4 cup) pine nuts
35 g (1/4 cup) currants
30 g (1/2 cup) chopped basil
2 tablespoons chopped
   flat-leaf (Italian) parsley
1 tablespoon chopped dill
olive oil, for brushing

Makes 8

Lightly oil a baking dish. Preheat the oven
to 160°C (315°F/Gas 2–3). Slice the top off
each tomato and reserve the tops. Spoon
out the flesh and put in a strainer to drain
the juice, reserving the juice. Finely dice the
flesh and reserve in a separate bowl. Drain
the tomato shells upside down on a rack.

Cook the rice in a saucepan of lightly salted,
rapidly boiling water for 10–12 minutes, or
until just tender. Drain and set aside to cool.

Heat the olive oil in a frying pan. Fry the
onion, garlic and oregano for 8 minutes, or
until the onion is tender. Add the pine
nuts and currants, and cook for 5 minutes,
stirring frequently. Remove from the heat
and stir in the fresh herbs. Season, to taste,
with salt and freshly ground black pepper.

Add the onion mixture and reserved
tomato flesh to the rice. Mix well. Fill the
tomato shells with the rice mixture, piling
it up over the top. Spoon 1 tablespoon of
the reserved tomato juice on top of each
tomato and replace the tomato tops.

Lightly brush the tomatoes with the olive
oil and arrange them in a baking dish.
Bake for 20–30 minutes, or until cooked
and heated through. Serve warm or cold.

chicken jambalaya

A speciality of Louisiana, USA, this Spanish-Creole dish uses a spicy blend of ingredients brought over by the colonists. Its name is thought to mean a mixture of *jamon* (ham) and paella. In this recipe, chicken has replaced the ham, but you can use both, if you prefer.

1/2 teaspoon ground white pepper
1/2 teaspoon ground black pepper
1/4 teaspoon cayenne pepper
500 g (1 lb 2 oz) chicken thigh fillets, each cut into 4 pieces
2 tablespoons vegetable oil
250 g (9 oz) chorizo, cut into 1 cm (1/4 in) slices
1 large onion, chopped
2 celery stalks, sliced
1 large green capsicum (pepper), chopped
4 garlic cloves, crushed
400 g (14 oz) tin chopped tomatoes
2 bay leaves
1/4 teaspoon Tabasco
200 g (1 cup) long- or medium-grain rice
875 ml (3 1/2 cups) hot chicken stock
450 g (1 lb) raw prawns (shrimp), peeled
3 tablespoons chopped fresh parsley

Serves 6

Put the white and black pepper, cayenne and 3/4 teaspoon salt in a bowl. Add the chicken thigh fillets and mix thoroughly to completely coat the chicken.

Heat the vegetable oil in a wide frying pan over medium heat and cook the chorizo for 5–6 minutes, or until lightly browned. Remove with a slotted spoon, leaving as much oil in the pan as possible. Add the chicken to the pan in batches and cook over medium heat for 6–8 minutes, until lightly browned, adding a little more oil if necessary. Remove the chicken from the pan with a slotted spoon, leaving as much fat in the pan as possible.

Add the onion, celery, capsicum and garlic to the pan, and cook over medium heat for 8 minutes, stirring often with a wooden spoon to lift the scrapings from the base of the pan. When the vegetables begin to brown, add the tomato, bay leaves and Tabasco, and simmer for 2–3 minutes.

Return the chorizo and chicken to the pan. Add the rice, stir briefly and add the stock. Don't stir at this point. Reduce the heat and simmer, uncovered, for 25–30 minutes, or until all the liquid has been absorbed and the rice is tender. Add the prawns and remove from the heat. Cover and leave for 10 minutes, so the prawns can cook in the residual heat. Then fluff up the rice with a fork, season well and stir in the parsley.

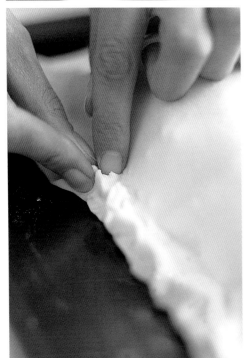

coulibiac

3 tablespoons butter
1 onion, finely chopped
200 g (7 oz) button mushrooms, sliced
2 tablespoons lemon juice
225 g (8 oz) salmon fillet, boned, skinned,
  cut into small cubes
2 hard-boiled eggs, chopped
2 tablespoons chopped dill
2 tablespoons chopped parsley
200 g (1 cup) cooked, cold
  long-grain rice
60 ml (1/4 cup) double thick cream
370 g (12 oz) block puff pastry
1 egg, lightly beaten

Serves 6

Melt half the butter in a frying pan, add the
onion and cook over medium heat until soft.
Add the mushrooms and cook for 5 minutes.
Stir in the juice and transfer to a bowl.

Melt the remaining butter in a pan, then
add the salmon and cook for 2 minutes.
Transfer to a bowl, cool slightly and add
the egg, dill and parsley. Season with salt
and pepper, combine gently and set aside.
In a small bowl, combine the rice and
cream, and season with salt and pepper.

Roll out half the pastry to an 18 x 30 cm
(7 x 12 in) rectangle and put it on the baking
tray. Spread half the rice mixture onto the
pastry, leaving a 3 cm (1 in) border all
around. Top with the salmon mixture, then
the mushrooms, and the remaining rice.

Roll out the remaining pastry to 20 x 32 cm
(8 x 13 in) and put it over the filling. Press
the pastry edges together, then crimp to
seal. Decorate with pastry cut-outs, if you
like, then refrigerate for 30 minutes.

Meanwhile, preheat the oven to hot 210°C
(415°F/Gas 6–7). Brush the pastry top with
the beaten egg and bake for 15 minutes.
Reduce the heat to 180°C (350°F/Gas 4)
and bake for another 15–20 minutes.

yangzhou fried rice with prawns

125 g (4 1/2 oz) cooked prawns (shrimp)
150 g (5 1/2 oz) fresh or frozen peas
1 tablespoon oil
3 spring onions (scallions), finely chopped
1 tablespoon finely chopped fresh ginger
2 eggs, lightly beaten
740 g (4 cups) cooked long-grain rice
1 1/2 tablespoons chicken stock
1 tablespoon Shaoxing rice wine
2 teaspoons light soy sauce
1/2 teaspoon roasted sesame oil
1/4 teaspoon freshly ground black pepper

Serves 4

Peel the prawns and, using a small, sharp knife, cut them in half through the back, removing the vein. Cook the peas in a saucepan of simmering water for about 3 minutes if fresh or 1 minute if frozen.

Heat a wok over high heat, then add the oil and heat until hot. Stir in the spring onion and ginger, and fry for 1 minute. Reduce the heat, add the egg and lightly scramble. Toss in the prawns and peas, and gently stir to heat through, then add the rice before the egg sets. Increase the heat and stir to separate the rice grains and break the egg into bits.

Add the stock, rice wine, light soy sauce, sesame oil, and 1/4 teaspoon each of salt and pepper. Toss lightly and serve.

egg fried rice

4 eggs
1 spring onion (scallion), chopped
50 g (1/3 cup) fresh or frozen peas (optional)
3 tablespoons oil
740 g (4 cups) cooked long-grain rice

Serves 4

Beat the eggs with a pinch of salt and 1 teaspoon of the spring onion. Cook the peas in a pan of simmering water for 3 minutes if fresh or 1 minute if frozen.

Heat a wok over high heat, add the oil and heat until very hot. Reduce the heat, add the egg and lightly scramble. Add the rice before the egg is completely set. Increase the heat, then stir to separate the rice grains and break the egg into small bits. Add the peas and the remaining spring onion, and season with salt. Stir constantly for 1 minute.

lamb pilaff

Countries of central Asia and the Middle East have a strong tradition of cooking pilaff—a dish which combines spice-seasoned rice, cooked in stock, with meat. There are endless variations but this recipe reflects the Persian preference for long-grain rice.

1 large eggplant (aubergine), cut into
   1 cm ($1/2$ in) cubes
125 ml ($1/2$ cup) olive oil
1 large onion, finely chopped
1 teaspoon ground cinnamon
2 teaspoons ground cumin
1 teaspoon ground coriander
300 g ($11/2$ cups) long-grain rice
500 ml (2 cups) chicken or
   vegetable stock
500 g (1 lb 2 oz) minced (ground) lamb
$1/2$ teaspoon allspice
2 tablespoons olive oil, extra
2 tomatoes, cut into wedges
3 tablespoons toasted pistachios
2 tablespoons currants
2 tablespoons chopped coriander
   (cilantro) leaves, to garnish

Serves 4

Put the eggplant in a colander, sprinkle generously with salt and leave for 1 hour. Rinse well and squeeze dry in a clean tea towel. Heat 2 tablespoons of the oil in a large, deep frying pan with a lid, add the eggplant and cook over medium heat for 8–10 minutes, or until golden and cooked through. Drain on paper towels.

Heat the remaining oil, add the onion and cook for 4–5 minutes, or until soft but not brown. Stir in half each of the cinnamon, cumin and coriander. Add the rice and stir to coat, then add the stock, season and bring to the boil. Reduce the heat and simmer, covered, for 15 minutes, adding more water if the pilaff starts to dry out.

Put the lamb in a bowl with the allspice and the remaining cumin, cinnamon and coriander. Season with salt and pepper, and mix well. Roll into balls the size of macadamia nuts. Heat the extra oil in the frying pan and cook the meatballs in batches over medium heat for 5 minutes each batch, or until lightly browned and cooked through. Drain on paper towels.

Add the tomato to the pan and cook, turning, for 3–5 minutes, or until lightly golden. Remove from the pan.

Stir the cooked eggplant, pistachios, currants and meatballs through the rice (this should be quite dry by now). Serve the pilaff surrounded by the cooked tomato and garnished with the coriander.

cinnamon sticks, cumin seeds and cloves are the secret spice agents in khichhari

khichhari

khichhari

60 g (2¹/4 oz) toor dal (yellow lentils)
300 g (1¹/2 cups) basmati rice
3 tablespoons ghee or unsalted butter
1 teaspoon cumin seeds
6 cloves
¹/2 cinnamon stick
2 onions, finely chopped
2 garlic cloves, finely chopped
2 cm (1 in) piece of fresh ginger, finely
  chopped
1 teaspoon garam masala
3 tablespoons lemon juice

Serves 6

Soak the dal in 500 ml (2 cups) of water in
a large saucepan for 2 hours. Wash the
rice in a sieve under cold, running water
until the water runs clear. Drain. Heat the
ghee in a heavy-based saucepan over low
heat and fry the cumin seeds, cloves and
cinnamon for a few seconds. Increase the
heat to medium, add the onion, garlic
and ginger, and cook until they soften and
begin to brown.

Add the rice and dal, and toss to
thoroughly coat in ghee. Add the garam
masala, lemon juice, 1 teaspoon of salt
and 750 ml (3 cups) of boiling water. Bring
to the boil, then reduce the heat to very
low, cover tightly and cook for 15 minutes.
Remove from the heat and gently fluff up
with a fork. Cover the pan with a clean
cloth and leave for 10 minutes. Fluff up
again and season with salt.

spicy portuguese chicken soup

2.5 litres (10 cups) chicken stock
1 onion, cut into thin wedges
1 celery stalk, finely chopped
1 teaspoon grated lemon zest
3 tomatoes, peeled, seeded and chopped
1 sprig mint
1 tablespoon olive oil
2 chicken breast fillets
200 g (1 cup) long-grain rice
2 tablespoons lemon juice
2 tablespoons shredded mint

Serves 6

Combine the chicken stock, onion, celery,
lemon zest, tomatoes, mint and olive oil in
a large saucepan. Slowly bring to the boil,
then reduce the heat, add the chicken and
simmer gently for 20–25 minutes, or until
the chicken is cooked through.

Remove the chicken from the saucepan
and discard the mint sprig. Allow the
chicken to cool, then thinly slice.

Meanwhile, add the rice to the pan and
simmer for 25–30 minutes, or until the rice
is tender. Return the sliced chicken to
the pan, add the lemon juice and stir for
1–2 minutes, or until the chicken is
warmed through. Season with salt and
pepper, and stir through the mint.

cabbage rolls

1 tablespoon olive oil
1 onion, finely chopped
large pinch of allspice
1 teaspoon ground cumin
large pinch of ground nutmeg
2 bay leaves
1 large head of cabbage
500 g (1 lb 2 oz) minced (ground) lamb
200 g (1 cup) long or medium-grain rice
4 cloves garlic, crushed
50 g (1/3 cup) toasted pine nuts
2 tablespoons chopped mint
2 tablespoons chopped flat-leaf
   (Italian) parsley
1 tablespoon chopped currants
250 ml (1 cup) olive oil, extra
80 ml (1/3 cup) lemon juice
extra virgin olive oil, to drizzle
lemon wedges, to serve

Makes 12 large rolls

Heat the oil in a saucepan, add the onion and cook over medium heat for 10 minutes, or until golden. Add the allspice, cumin and nutmeg, and cook for 2 minutes, or until fragrant. Remove from the pan.

Bring a large saucepan of water to the boil and add the bay leaves. Cut the tough outer leaves and about 5 cm (2 in) of the core from the cabbage, then carefully add the cabbage to the boiling water. Cook it for 5 minutes, then carefully loosen a whole leaf with tongs and remove. Continue to cook and remove the leaves until you reach the core. Drain, reserving the cooking liquid, and set aside to cool.

Take 12 leaves of about equal size and cut a small 'V' from the core end of each to remove the thickest part. Trim the firm central veins so the leaf is as flat as possible. Put three-quarters of the remaining leaves on the base of a large saucepan to prevent the rolls catching.

Combine the mince, onion mixture, rice, garlic, pine nuts, mint, parsley and currants in a bowl. Season well. With the core end of the leaf closest to you, form 2 tablespoons of the mixture into an oval and put it in the centre of the leaf. Roll up, tucking in the sides. Repeat with the remaining 11 leaves and filling. Put the rolls, seam-side-down, in a single layer in the lined saucepan, to fit snugly.

Combine 625 ml (2 1/2 cups) of the cooking liquid with the extra olive oil, lemon juice and 1 teaspoon of salt, and pour over the rolls (the liquid should just come to the top of the rolls). Lay the remaining leaves over the top. Cover with a lid and bring to the boil over high heat, then reduce the heat. Simmer for 1 hour and 15 minutes, or until the mince and rice are cooked. Carefully remove the rolls from the pan with a slotted spoon, then drizzle with extra virgin olive oil. Serve with lemon wedges.

saffron chicken and rice

Saffron, a spice extracted from the crocus plant, gives rice dishes a great colour and aromatic flavour. It has always been the most expensive of spices, but only a little is needed as it goes a long way. The best quality saffron comes from Spain, Iran and Kashmir.

60 ml (1/4 cup) olive oil
4 chicken thighs and 6 drumsticks
1 large red onion, finely chopped
1 large green capsicum (pepper),
  two-thirds diced and one-third julienned
3 teaspoons sweet paprika
400 g (14 oz) tin diced tomatoes
250 g (11/4 cups) long-grain rice
1/2 teaspoon ground saffron

Serves 4

Heat 2 tablespoons of the oil in a deep frying pan over high heat. Season the chicken pieces well and brown in batches. Remove the chicken from the pan.

Reduce the heat to medium and add the remaining oil. Add the onion and diced capsicum, and cook gently for 5 minutes. Stir in the paprika and cook for about 30 seconds. Add the tomato and simmer for 1–3 minutes, until the mixture thickens.

Stir 875 ml (31/2 cups) of boiling water into the pan, then add the rice and saffron. Return the chicken to the pan and stir to combine. Season with salt and pepper. Bring to the boil, cover, reduce the heat to medium–low and simmer for 20 minutes, or until all the liquid has been absorbed and the chicken is tender. Stir in the julienned capsicum, then allow it to stand, covered, for 3–4 minutes before serving.

avgolemono soup with chicken

1 onion, halved
2 cloves
1 carrot, cut into chunks
1 bay leaf
500 g (1 lb 2 oz) chicken breast fillets
65 g (1/3 cup) long- or medium-grain rice
3 eggs, separated
3 tablespoons lemon juice
2 tablespoons chopped flat-leaf
   (Italian) parsley

Serves 4

Stud the onion with the cloves and put it in a large saucepan with 1.5 litres (6 cups) of water. Add the carrot, bay leaf and chicken, and season with salt and freshly ground black pepper. Slowly bring to the boil, then reduce the heat and simmer for 10 minutes, or until the chicken is cooked.

Strain the stock into a clean saucepan, reserving the chicken and discarding the vegetables. Add the rice to the stock, bring to the boil, then reduce the heat and simmer for 15 minutes, or until the rice is tender. Tear the chicken into shreds.

Whisk the egg whites in a clean dry bowl until stiff peaks form, then beat in the yolks. Slowly beat in the lemon juice. Gently stir in 170 ml (2/3 cup) of the hot (not boiling) stock and beat thoroughly. Add the egg mixture to the stock and heat gently, but do not boil as the eggs may scramble. Add the chicken and season with salt and black pepper.

Set the soup aside for 3 minutes to allow the flavours to develop, then sprinkle the parsley over the top and serve.

hopping john

300 g (10 1/2 oz) black-eyed beans
4 bacon rashers, rinds removed
1 tablespoon oil
1 onion, finely chopped
1 red capsicum (pepper), finely chopped
100 g (1/2 cup) long-grain rice
Louisiana hot sauce or chilli sauce

Serves 4

Soak the black-eyed beans in cold water overnight, then drain. Dice the bacon rashers and fry them in the oil with the onion and red capsicum until the bacon is crisp and the vegetables are soft.

Add the beans, rice and 500 ml (2 cups) of water. Cover, bring to the boil and simmer for about 20 minutes, or until the rice is cooked. Season the dish with salt, black pepper and some Louisiana hot sauce.

nasi goreng (fried rice)

In Malay, *nasi* means 'cooked rice' and *goreng* 'fried', but there is more to this recipe than fried rice. It is a Dutch–Indonesian dish in which a selection of ingredients, including any type of meat and seafood, is added to the rice, along with slices of omelette.

2 eggs
80 ml ($1/3$ cup) oil
3 garlic cloves, finely chopped
1 onion, finely chopped
2 red chillies, seeded and very
  finely chopped
1 teaspoon shrimp paste
1 teaspoon coriander seeds
$1/2$ teaspoon sugar
400 g (14 oz) raw prawns (shrimp), peeled
  and deveined
200 g (7 oz) rump steak, finely sliced
200 g (1 cup) long-grain rice, cooked
  and cooled
2 teaspoons kecap manis
1 tablespoon soy sauce
4 spring onions (scallions), finely chopped
$1/2$ lettuce, finely shredded
1 cucumber, thinly sliced
3 tablespoons crisp fried onion

Serves 4

Beat the eggs and $1/4$ teaspoon of salt until foamy. Heat a frying pan and lightly brush with a little of the oil. Pour about one-quarter of the egg mixture into the pan and cook for 1–2 minutes over medium heat, or until the omelette sets. Turn the omelette over and cook the other side for about 30 seconds. Remove the omelette from the pan and repeat with the remaining egg mixture. When the omelettes are cold, gently roll them up, cut into fine strips and set aside.

Combine the garlic, onion, chilli, shrimp paste, coriander and sugar in a food processor or mortar and pestle, and process or pound until a paste is formed.

Heat 1–2 tablespoons of the oil in a wok or large, deep frying pan; add the paste and cook over high heat for 1 minute, or until fragrant. Add the prawns and steak, and stir-fry for 2–3 minutes, or until the prawns and steak change colour.

Add the remaining oil and the cold rice to the wok. Stir-fry, breaking up any lumps, until the rice is heated through. Add the kecap manis, soy sauce and spring onion, and stir-fry for another minute.

Arrange the lettuce around the outside of a large platter. Put the rice in the centre, and garnish with the omelette, cucumber slices and fried onion. Serve immediately.

fresh, briny mussels play a main role in thai seafood cooking

green-lip mussels in coconut milk

green-lip mussels in coconut milk

4 shallots, peeled
1 large garlic clove, peeled
1 stem lemon grass, white part
  roughly chopped
2 cm (1 in) piece fresh ginger, peeled and
  roughly chopped
1–2 small red chillies, cut in half
  lengthways and seeded
3 tablespoons olive oil
400 ml (14 fl oz) tin coconut milk
zest of 1 lime
4 tablespoons of lime juice
1 tablespoon Thai fish sauce
1.8 kg (4 lb) green-lip mussels, in the
  shell, cleaned
100 g ($1/2$ cup) long-grain rice
1 tablespoon chopped coriander
  (cilantro) leaves
1 tablespoon chopped basil leaves

Serves 4

Whiz the shallots, garlic, lemon grass, ginger
and chilli together in a food processor until
finely chopped. Alternatively, finely chop
the ingredients and mix by hand. Heat the
oil in a large saucepan and add the shallot
mixture. Cook, stirring for 2 minutes, then
add the coconut milk, lime zest, juice and
fish sauce, and simmer for 2 minutes.

Add the mussels, bring to the boil and
cover with a lid. Cook for 7 minutes, shaking
the saucepan. The mussels will open when
cooked—discard any that do not open.

Drain the mussels in a colander over a large
bowl, reserving the coconut liquid, and
rinse the saucepan. Pass the reserved liquid
through a sieve. Return the liquid to the
pan with the rice and 125 ml ($1/2$ cup) water,
bring to the boil and simmer for 8 minutes
or until the rice is cooked. Add the herbs.
Ladle the coconut rice into bowls and
evenly divide the mussels. For effect, try to
have the green lips of the mussels showing.

congee

200 g (1 cup) long-grain rice
2.25 litres (9 cups) chicken stock
light soy sauce
sesame oil

toppings

3 spring onions (scallions), chopped
4 tablespoons chopped coriander
  (cilantro) leaves
2 tablespoons sliced pickled ginger
4 tablespoons finely chopped
  preserved turnip
4 tablespoons roasted peanuts
2 one-thousand-year-old eggs, cut
  into slivers
2 tablespoons toasted sesame seeds
2 fried dough sticks, diagonally sliced

Serves 4

Put the rice in a bowl and, using your
fingers as a rake, rinse under cold running
water to remove any dust. Drain the rice in
a colander. Put it in a clay pot, casserole
or saucepan and stir in the stock or water.
Bring to the boil, then reduce the heat
and allow to simmer very gently, stirring
occasionally, for $13/4$–2 hours, or until
it has a porridge-like texture and the rice
is breaking up.

Add a sprinkling of soy sauce, sesame oil
and white pepper to season the congee.
You can serve the congee plain, or choose
a selection of toppings from those listed
above and serve in bowls alongside the
congee for guests to help themselves.

tandoori chicken with cardamom rice

250 ml (1 cup) plain yoghurt, plus
   extra for serving
60 g (¹/₄ cup) tandoori paste
2 tablespoons lemon juice
1 kg (2 lb 4 oz) chicken breast fillets,
   cut into 4 cm (1¹/₂ in) cubes
1 tablespoon oil
1 onion, finely diced
300 g (1¹/₂ cups) long-grain rice
2 cardamom pods, bruised
750 ml (3 cups) hot chicken stock
400 g (14 oz) English spinach leaves

Serves 4

Soak eight wooden skewers in water for
30 minutes to prevent them burning during
cooking. Combine the yoghurt, tandoori
paste and lemon juice in a non-metallic
dish. Add the chicken and coat well, then
cover and marinate for at least 10 minutes.

Meanwhile, heat the oil in a saucepan. Add
the onion and cook for 3 minutes, then
add the rice and cardamom pods. Cook,
stirring often, for 3–5 minutes, or until the
rice is slightly opaque. Add the hot chicken
stock and bring to the boil. Reduce the
heat to low, cover, and cook the rice,
without removing the lid, for 15 minutes.

Heat a barbecue plate or oven grill to very
hot. Thread the chicken cubes onto the
skewers, leaving the bottom quarter of
the skewers empty. Cook on each side for
4–5 minutes, or until cooked through.

Wash the spinach and put it in a large
saucepan with just the water clinging to
the leaves. Cook, covered, over medium
heat for 1–2 minutes, or until the spinach
has wilted. Uncover the rice, fluff up with
a fork and serve with the spinach, chicken
and extra yoghurt.

arroz con mariscos

The Mexican version of paella includes firm-fleshed fish and a unique, delicious flavour derived from roasting the base ingredients before adding them to the sauce.

1 large garlic clove, peeled
1 onion, peeled and quartered
2 firm tomatoes
1 red capsicum (pepper), seeded
   and quartered
3 tablespoons olive oil
55 g (2 oz) bacon, chopped
265 g (1¹/3 cups) long-grain rice
625 ml (2¹/2 cups) hot fish stock or water
250 g (9 oz) firm fish, such as snapper,
   skinned and cut into chunks
2 tinned and drained, or fresh, poblanos
   chillies, finely shredded
16 raw tiger prawns (shrimp), peeled and
   deveined, tails intact
2 tablespoons chopped coriander
   (cilantro) leaves
1 lime, cut into 4 wedges

Serves 4

Begin by dry-roasting the garlic, onion, tomato and capsicum in a heavy-based frying pan over a low heat until the ingredients are browned all over. Turn now and then—the skins of the tomato and capsicum will blacken and blister, making it easy to peel them. The browning will take between 40 and 45 minutes.

When cool enough to handle, peel the tomato and capsicum, and roughly chop. Put in a food processor with the garlic and onion, and blend to a purée. Alternatively, finely chop the ingredients by hand.

Heat the olive oil in a deep frying pan. Add the bacon and cook until crisp. Add the rice and cook for 1 minute, stirring the grains to make sure they are completely coated in oil.

Add the puréed tomato and cook for 3 minutes. Add the stock and 1 teaspoon of salt. Bring to the boil and stir once. Reduce the heat to low and cover with a lid. Cook gently for 15 minutes.

Cut the fish into chunks. Add the chillies, prawns and fish to the frying pan, and cook for another 5 minutes. Add a little hot water to the rice if it is becoming too dry. When ready, taste to check the seasoning, adding more salt if necessary.

Sprinkle the coriander over the top of the dish and serve with the lime wedges.

fragrant lemon grass rice and prawns

5 garlic cloves, peeled
4 cm (1 1/2 in) piece of fresh ginger,
   peeled and chopped
3 coriander (cilantro) roots, washed
   thoroughly
2 long green chillies, seeded
   and chopped
1 onion, peeled and chopped
2 tablespoons lime juice
1 teaspoon palm sugar
3 tablespoons oil
2 stalks lemon grass (white part
   only), bruised
4 makrut (kaffir) lime leaves
700 g (1 lb 9 oz) medium raw prawns
   (shrimp), peeled and deveined
400 g (2 cups) long-grain rice, washed
   and drained
250 ml (1 cup) fish stock
100 g (3 1/2 oz) snake beans, cut into
   3 cm (1 1/4 in) lengths
1 Lebanese (short) cucumber
2 tablespoons fresh coriander (cilantro)
   leaves, to garnish
2 tablespoons fried red Asian
   shallot flakes

Serves 4

In the small bowl of a food processor, add the garlic, ginger, coriander roots, green chillies and onion. Add 2–3 tablespoons of water, and blend to a smooth paste.

In a small separate bowl, combine the lime juice and palm sugar, stirring until the sugar is dissolved. Set aside.

In a heavy-based, deep frying pan with a tight-fitting lid, heat half the oil on medium heat. Add the prepared paste, lemon grass and lime leaves, and cook for 5 minutes or until the mixture is soft and fragrant, taking care not to brown it. Add the prawns and cook for 2 minutes, or until pink. Remove with a slotted spoon and set aside.

Add rice to the pan, stir for 1 minute to coat well, then add fish stock and 500 ml (2 cups) of water, and stir well. Increase the heat to high and bring to the boil. Stir in the beans and lime juice mixture, then season well with salt. Cover with a lid and simmer over low heat for 15–20 minutes, or until most of the water is absorbed. Meanwhile, cut the cucumber in half, lengthways, remove the seeds and dice.

When most of the water is absorbed, reduce the heat to very low, stir through the prawns, then replace the lid and cook for an additional 5 minutes, or until the rice is tender and the prawns are cooked through. Let the rice stand, covered, for 5 minutes before fluffing up with a fork. Discard the lemon grass stalks and makrut lime leaves. Serve sprinkled with the diced cucumber, whole coriander leaves and fried red Asian shallot flakes.

eggplant is the star fruit of many mediterranean dishes

baked eggplant

baked eggplant

185 ml (3/4 cup) olive oil
2 large eggplants (aubergines),
  cut in half lengthways
3 onions, thinly sliced
3 garlic cloves, finely chopped
400 g (14 oz) Roma (plum) tomatoes,
  peeled and chopped, or a 400 g (14 oz)
  tin of good-quality chopped tomatoes
2 teaspoons dried oregano
4 tablespoons chopped flat-leaf
  (Italian) parsley
35 g (1/4 cup) currants
1/4 teaspoon ground cinnamon
185 g (1 cup) long-grain rice, cooked and
  drained
2 tablespoons lemon juice
pinch of sugar
125 ml (1/2 cup) tomato juice

Serves 4

Preheat the oven to 180°C (350°F/Gas 4).
Heat half the oil in a heavy-based frying
pan and cook the eggplants on all sides
for 8–10 minutes, until the cut sides are
golden. Remove from the pan and scoop
out some of the flesh, leaving the skins
intact and some of the flesh lining the
skin. Finely chop the flesh and set aside.

Heat the remaining olive oil in the same
frying pan and cook the onion over
medium heat for 8–10 minutes, or until
transparent. Add the garlic and cook for
another minute. Add the tomato, oregano,
parsley, currants, cinnamon, rice and the
eggplant. Season with salt and pepper.

Put the eggplant shells in an ovenproof
dish and fill each with the prepared
tomato mixture. In a bowl, mix the lemon
juice, sugar, tomato juice and some salt,
and pour over the eggplant. Cover and
bake for 30 minutes, then uncover and
cook for another 10 minutes. Serve
eggplants on a platter with a light drizzle
of oil and any of the remaining juice.

thai basil fried rice

2 tablespoons oil
3 Asian shallots, sliced
1 garlic clove, finely chopped
1 small fresh red chilli, finely chopped
100 g (31/2 oz) snake or green beans, cut
  into short pieces
1 small red capsicum (pepper), cut
  into batons
90 g (31/2 oz) button mushrooms, halved
470 g (21/2 cups) cooked jasmine rice
1 teaspoon grated palm sugar
3 tablespoons light soy sauce
10 g (1/4 cup) fresh Thai basil, shredded
1 tablespoon coriander (cilantro)
  leaves, chopped
fried red Asian shallot flakes, to garnish
Thai basil leaves, to garnish

Serves 4

Heat a wok over high heat, add the oil and
swirl. Stir-fry the shallots, garlic and chilli
for 3 minutes, or until the shallots start to
brown. Add the beans, capsicum and
mushrooms, stir-fry for 3 minutes, or until
cooked, then stir in the cooked jasmine rice
and heat through.

Dissolve the palm sugar in the soy sauce,
then pour over the rice. Stir in the herbs.
Garnish with the shallot flakes and basil.

steamed stuffed mussels
(homok hoie man poo)

Eating Thai food without rice is unthinkable. Rice is the life force of the meal—any other dish merely acts as a flavouring. Wet dishes, like this one, serve to dress and moisten the rice. The aromatic jasmine grain has been used in this fresh and fragrant seafood recipe.

2 kg (4 lb 8 oz) black mussels
125 ml ($1/2$ cup) white wine
3 garlic cloves, chopped
4 fresh coriander (cilantro) roots
1 stem lemon grass
1 lime, sliced
2 small red onions, chopped
1 tablespoon peanut oil
200 g (1 cup) jasmine rice
80 g ($1/2$ cup) roasted unsalted
   peanuts, chopped
2 teaspoons finely chopped fresh ginger
1 tablespoon fish sauce
1 tablespoon tamarind purée
20 g ($1/3$ cup) fresh coriander (cilantro)
   leaves, chopped
4 fresh makrut (kaffir) lime leaves,
   shredded
fresh Vietnamese mint, shredded,
   to garnish

Serves 6

Scrub the mussels with a stiff brush and remove the beards. Discard any mussels which are broken or don't close when tapped. Rinse well. Put the mussels in a large bamboo steamer and cover.

Put the wine, 375 ml ($11/2$ cups) of water, two of the garlic cloves, the coriander roots, the green part of the lemon grass stalk, the lime slices and half the onion in a wok. Bring to a simmer.

Sit the steamer over the wok and steam for 5–6 minutes, or until the mussels open. Discard any that have not opened. Remove and discard the upper shell. Strain the mussels and reserve the liquid.

Heat the oil in a wok over medium heat. Add the remaining onion and garlic, the finely chopped white part of the lemon grass stalk and the rice, and stir-fry for 2–3 minutes, or until the onion is soft. Add 500 ml (2 cups) of the reserved liquid and simmer for 20 minutes. Preheat the oven to 200°C (400°F/Gas 6).

Toss in the peanuts, ginger, fish sauce, tamarind, coriander and lime leaves.

Spoon the mixture onto each shell half, transfer to an ovenproof baking dish and bake for 10 minutes. Garnish with the shredded mint and serve immediately.

chicken biryani

This is another interpretation of the famous Indian recipe. The rice and highly spiced chicken are cooked in layers in a covered dish to keep in the flavours. Though biryani is traditionally served on festive occasions, it's good enough to eat as a regular treat.

800 g (4 cups) basmati rice
3 onions, sliced
125 ml ($1/2$ cup) oil
180 g ($3/4$ cup) ghee or unsalted butter
4 cm ($1 1/2$ in) piece cinnamon stick
2 cardamom pods
3 cloves
2 star anise
2 stalks of curry leaves
2 cm ($3/4$ in) piece of fresh ginger, grated
6 garlic cloves, crushed
1.3 kg (3 lb) chicken pieces
4–6 green chillies, slit lengthways
500 ml (2 cups) buttermilk
4 ripe tomatoes, diced
185 ml ($3/4$ cup) coconut milk
1 litre (4 cups) chicken stock
1 lemon, cut into wedges

Serves 8

Wash the rice in a sieve under cold, running water until the water runs clear. Drain well. Put the sliced onion in a sieve, sprinkle with $1/2$ teaspoon of salt and leave for 10 minutes to drain off any liquid that oozes out. Rinse and pat dry.

Heat the oil and ghee over medium heat in a large, heavy-based ovenproof casserole. Add the cinnamon, cardamom and cloves, and heat until they begin to crackle. Reduce the heat to low and add the star anise and the curry leaves from one stalk. Stir in the sliced onion and cook until golden brown. Toss in the ginger and garlic, and cook until golden.

Mix in the chicken, increase the heat to medium and fry until the pieces are browned on all sides. Add the chillies, the remaining curry leaves, buttermilk and some salt. Cook for 12 minutes, or until the chicken is cooked through and the liquid is reduced by half. Stir in the diced tomato and the coconut milk. Cook until the tomato is tender, then pour in the stock and bring to the boil.

Preheat the oven to 220°C (425°F/Gas 7). Add the drained rice to the chicken and stir well. Check the seasoning, adjust if necessary, and cook for 10 minutes, or until most of the liquid is absorbed.

Remove the pot from the heat, cover with a clean wet cloth, then a tight-fitting lid, and put the pot in the oven for 15 minutes, or until the rice is cooked through. Serve hot with lemon wedges.

moroccan stuffed sardines

100 g (¹/2 cup) long-grain rice
2 tablespoons olive oil
25 g (1 oz) ready-to-eat dried apricots,
   chopped into small pieces
25 g (1 oz) raisins
1 tablespoon flaked toasted almonds
1 tablespoon chopped parsley
1 tablespoon chopped mint
grated zest of 1 orange
2 tablespoons freshly squeezed
   orange juice
1 teaspoon finely chopped
   preserved lemon
1 teaspoon ground cinnamon
¹/2 teaspoon harissa
16 whole large sardines, butterflied
16 large fresh vine leaves or preserved
   vine leaves
250 ml (1 cup) plain Greek-style yoghurt,
   to serve

Makes 16

Cook the rice in boiling water until it is
tender. Drain and transfer to a bowl. Add
1 tablespoon of the olive oil, the apricots,
raisins, almonds, parsley, mint, orange zest
and juice, preserved lemon, cinnamon, harissa
and the second tablespoon of oil. Season with
salt and pepper, and mix together.

Divide the stuffing between the sardines,
folding the two fillets of each fish together to
enclose the rice mixture (save any extra
stuffing to serve with the sardines). Bring a
pan of water to the boil and, in batches,
blanch the vine leaves for 30 seconds at a
time. Pat dry on crumpled paper towels. If you
are using preserved vine leaves, rinse and dry
them. Wrap a vine leaf around each sardine
and secure with a toothpick.

Preheat a grill or barbecue. Cook the sardines
for 6 minutes, turning them over halfway
through. Serve each one with a dollop of
yoghurt and any extra rice.

zanzibar pilau with squid and prawns

This aromatic rice dish is redolent of the rich, warm flavours that infuse the food of Zanzibar—an archipelago in the Indian Ocean, off the coast of Tanzania. The wide use of wonderful, exotic spices is a legacy of the country's Arab heritage.

1 cinnamon stick
6 cloves
6 cardamom pods
1/2 teaspoon coriander seeds
1/2 teaspoon black peppercorns
3 tablespoons oil
2 onions, finely chopped
3 garlic cloves, finely chopped
2 teaspoons finely chopped
  fresh ginger
200 g (1 cup) long-grain rice
560 ml (2 1/4 cups) vegetable stock
3 tomatoes, chopped
150 g (5 1/2 oz) raisins
450 g (1 lb) baby squid, cleaned,
  tentacles left whole
450 g (1 lb) prawns, peeled and
  deveined, tails intact

Serves 6

Put the cinnamon, cloves, cardamom pods, coriander seeds and black peppercorns in a large cup or mug. Cover with about 300 ml (10 1/2 fl oz) of hot water. Set aside to infuse for at least 30 minutes.

Heat 2 tablespoons of the oil in a large sauté or frying pan and, when hot, add the onion. Cook over a medium heat for 10 minutes, stirring occasionally, until softened. Add the garlic and ginger, and cook for a further 2 minutes, stirring frequently. Add the rice and stir to coat with the oil. Add the spices, the infusing liquid and the stock, bring to the boil, then reduce the heat, cover the pan and cook for 5 minutes, stirring occasionally.

Add the tomato and raisins, cover the pan again and cook, stirring occasionally, for a further 8–10 minutes, or until the rice is tender. If the rice is drying out, add a little more boiling water. When the rice is cooked, season to taste, then remove the pan from the heat and set aside.

Cut open the squid tubes and halve or quarter them. Score a fine crisscross pattern on the inside of each tube, taking care not to cut the tube all the way through. Season the prawns and squid thoroughly with salt and pepper.

Heat the remaining tablespoon of oil in a frying pan and cook the prawns for about 2–3 minutes. Pile the pilau onto a serving dish and put the prawns on top.

Quickly cook the squid in the frying pan for 30–60 seconds on each side, adding a little more oil if necessary. Put it on top of the pilau and serve immediately.

dried mushrooms will keep in the pantry for years and are a great stand-by for chinese dishes

steamed chicken and sausage rice

steamed chicken and sausage rice

4 dried Chinese mushrooms
250 g (9 oz) skinless chicken thigh fillet
1 teaspoon Shaoxing rice wine
2 teaspoons cornflour
3 Chinese sausages (lap cheong)
200 g (1 cup) long-grain rice
1 spring onion (scallion), chopped

sauce
1 tablespoon Shaoxing rice wine
2 tablespoons light soy sauce
1/2 teaspoon caster (superfine) sugar
1/2 garlic clove, chopped
1/2 teaspoon chopped fresh ginger
1/2 teaspoon roasted sesame oil

Serves 4

Soak the mushrooms in boiling water for
30 minutes, then drain and squeeze out
any excess water. Remove and discard the
stems and shred the caps. Cut the chicken
into bite-size pieces and combine with a
pinch of salt, the rice wine and cornflour.
Put the sausages on a plate in a steamer.
Simmer, covered, over water in a wok, for
10 minutes. Cut into thin diagonal slices.

Put the rice in a bowl and, using your
fingers as a rake, rinse under cold running
water to remove any dust. Drain the rice in
a colander, put it in a clay pot or casserole,
or four individual clay pots, and add
enough water so there is 2 cm (3/4 in) of
water above the surface of the rice. Bring
the water slowly to the boil, stir, then
lay the chicken and mushrooms on the
rice. Top with the sausage slices. Cook,
covered, over very low heat for about
15–18 minutes, or until the rice is cooked.

To make the sauce, combine the rice wine,
soy sauce, sugar, garlic, ginger and sesame
oil in a saucepan and heat until almost
boiling. Pour the sauce over the chicken
and sausage, and add the spring onion.

salmon kedgeree

1 litre (4 cups) fish stock
400 g (14 oz) salmon fillet
3 tablespoons butter
2 tablespoons oil
1 onion, chopped
2 teaspoons madras curry paste
200 g (1 cup) long-grain rice
2 hard-boiled eggs, cut into wedges
3 tablespoons chopped parsley leaves
3 tablespoons cream
lemon wedges, to serve

Serves 4

Put the stock in a frying pan and bring to
the boil. Put the salmon in the stock, cover,
then reduce the heat to a simmer. Cook
for 3 minutes, or until it becomes firm
when pressed and turns opaque. Lift out
the salmon and flake it into large pieces
by gently pulling it apart with your hands.

Melt half of the butter in a frying pan with
the oil, add the onion and cook over a
low heat until the onion softens and turns
translucent. Stir in the curry paste, then
add the rice and mix well until the rice is
coated. Add the fish stock, mix well, then
bring the mixture to the boil.

Simmer the rice, covered, over a very low
heat for 8 minutes, then add the salmon
and cook, covered, for another 5 minutes,
until all the liquid is absorbed. If the rice
is too dry and not cooked, add a splash of
boiling water and keep cooking for a
further 1–2 minutes.

Stir in the rest of the butter, the eggs,
parsley and cream (you can leave out the
cream if you prefer—the results won't be
so rich). Serve the kedgeree with the
lemon wedges to squeeze over.

senegal fish stew

In Senegal, West Africa, *diebou dien*, or fish stew with rice, is the national dish. As it is common for local fishermen to dry part of their catch, the stew combines both fresh and dried fish. If dried fish is unavailable, or you don't have time to soak it, just leave it out.

115 g (4 oz) dried white fish, such
  as salted cod
6 tablespoons oil
3 tablespoons chopped parsley
1 1/2 teaspoons crushed dried chilli
5 large garlic cloves, crushed
6 x 150 g (5 1/2 oz) mixed white
  fish steaks
2 onions, chopped
3 tablespoons tomato passata
1.5 litres (6 cups) well-flavoured fish stock
400 g (2 cups) long-grain rice
400 g (14 oz) orange-fleshed sweet
  potato, peeled and cut into chunks
150 g (5 1/2 oz) carrot, peeled and cut
  into chunks
1 red capsicum (pepper), seeded and
  cut into chunks
300 g (10 1/2 oz) white cabbage, cut
  into chunks

Serves 4

Soak the dried fish in water overnight, changing the water three to four times. Put it in a saucepan with clean water and simmer for 15–20 minutes or until soft. Drain and remove any skin and bones.

Mix together 3 tablespoons of the oil with 2 tablespoons of the parsley, half a teaspoon of the dried chilli and three of the crushed garlic cloves. Rub into the fresh fish, transfer to a non-metallic dish, cover and refrigerate for 30 minutes.

Heat a tablespoon of the remaining oil in a large saucepan and add the onion. Cook for 5–7 minutes, or until the onion has softened. Stir in the remaining garlic and cook for a further minute. Add the tomato passata and remaining teaspoon of dried chilli to the cooked onions, then pour in the stock. Season with salt, bring to the boil, then gently simmer for 10 minutes.

Meanwhile, heat a frying pan with the remaining 2 tablespoons of oil and cook the fresh fish for 1 minute on each side. Transfer to a plate and set aside. Tip the rice into a saucepan. Add 800 ml (28 fl oz) of water and a generous pinch of salt. Bring the liquid back to the boil, then reduce the heat to low. Cover and cook for 15 minutes or until tender.

Stir the sweet potato and carrot into the stew, and simmer for 10 minutes. Add the capsicum, cabbage and dried fish. Simmer for 5 minutes, season and add more dried chilli, if desired. Put the fish steaks on top and cook, covered, for 6 minutes or until the fish is cooked through. Scatter with the remaining parsley. Drain the cooked rice and serve with the fish.

nasi lemak

Traditionally served for breakfast in Malaysia, this hearty hotpot of contrasting tastes is now enjoyed at any time. Its main component, fragrant rice cooked in coconut milk, is served with a spicy, pungent prawn paste called sambal—the crowning glory of the dish.

rice

300 g (1 1/2 cups) long-grain rice
2 Asian shallots
2 slices fresh ginger
pinch fenugreek seeds
400 ml (14 fl oz) tin coconut milk
2 pandanus leaves, knotted

sambal ikan bilis

3 tablespoons oil
5 Asian shallots
2 garlic cloves
1 stem lemon grass (white part only),
    thinly sliced
1/2 teaspoon shrimp paste
2 tablespoons chilli paste
100 g (3 1/2 oz) ikan bilis, soaked
    and washed
1 teaspoon sugar
2 tablespoons lime juice

rendang

2 onions, roughly chopped
2 garlic cloves, crushed
400 ml (14 fl oz) tin coconut milk
2 teaspoons ground coriander seeds
1/2 teaspoon ground fennel seeds
2 teaspoons ground cumin seeds
1/4 teaspoon ground cloves
1.5 kg (3 lb 5 oz) chuck steak, cut
    into cubes
4–6 small red chillies, chopped
1 tablespoon lemon juice
1 stem lemon grass (white part only),
    bruised and cut lengthways
2 teaspoons grated palm sugar or
    soft brown sugar

Serves 4

Put the rice, shallots, ginger, fenugreek and 1 teaspoon of salt in a rice cooker. Pour enough coconut milk over the rice so so there is 2 cm (3/4 in) of liquid above the surface of the rice. Cook until dry, then fluff up the grains. Sprinkle the rest of the coconut milk over the rice. Stir to evenly distribute the milk. Stand for 15 minutes, until the coconut milk is absorbed.

To make the sambal, heat the oil in a wok, add the shallots, garlic, lemon grass, shrimp paste and chilli paste, and stir-fry until fragrant. Add the ikan bilis and the onion, and stir-fry to combine. Mix in the sugar and the lime juice.

In a food processor, process the onion, garlic and 1 tablespoon of water to form a smooth paste.

To make the rendang, put the coconut milk in a wok and bring to the boil, then reduce the heat to medium and cook, stirring occasionally, for 15 minutes, or until the milk is reduced by half and the oil has separated. Do not allow the milk to brown. Add the coriander, fennel and cumin seeds, and the ground cloves to the pan, and stir for 1 minute. Add the steak and cook for 2 minutes, or until it changes colour. Add the prepared onion mixture, chilli, lemon juice, lemon grass and sugar. Cook, covered, over medium heat for about 2 hours, or until the liquid is reduced and thickened. Stir frequently.

Uncover and continue cooking until the oil separates again. Take care not to burn the curry sauce. The curry is cooked when it is brown and dry. Serve the prepared rice with the rendang and sambal.

red beans and rice

Commonly called 'red and white', this southern American dish is traditionally served on Mondays. The reasons why are left to folklore—either it was easy to prepare on wash day; it made good use of Sunday's leftover ham; or it soaked up the alcohol from the weekend.

210 g (1 cup) red kidney beans
2 tablespoons oil
1 onion, finely chopped
1 green capsicum (pepper), chopped
3 celery stalks, finely chopped
2 garlic cloves, crushed
225 g (8 oz) andouille or other spicy
   sausage, cut into pieces
2 ham hocks
2 bay leaves
200 g (1 cup) long-grain rice
5 spring onions (scallions), finely sliced,
   to garnish

Serves 4

Soak the red kidney beans overnight in cold water. Drain and put into a saucepan with enough cold water to cover the beans. Bring to the boil, then reduce the heat to a simmer.

Heat the oil in a frying pan and sauté the onion, capsicum, celery and garlic until soft. Add the sausage and sauté until it begins to brown around the edges.

Add the sautéed vegetables and sausage to the beans along with the ham and bay leaves. Bring to the boil, then reduce to a simmer and cook for $2^1/2$–3 hours, adding more water if necessary—the beans should be saucy but not too liquid. When the beans are almost cooked, boil the rice in a separate saucepan until it is tender.

Top the cooked rice with the red kidney beans. Tear some meat off the ham hocks and add to each serving plate. Garnish with the sliced spring onions.

sticky rice with mangoes

Asian-style rice puddings are proof of the super grain's versatility. Prepared using sweet, luscious coconut milk, this sticky rice dessert has a rich, comforting texture and dreamy taste which is rounded out with the refreshing fruity flavour of tropical mango.

400 g (2 cups) long-grain glutinous rice
1 tablespoon white sesame seeds, to serve
250 ml (1 cup) coconut milk
90 g (1/2 cup) grated palm sugar or soft brown sugar
2–3 mangoes, peeled, seeded and sliced
3 tablespoons coconut cream
mint sprigs, to garnish

Serves 4

Put the rice in a sieve and wash under cold running water until the water runs clear. Put the rice in a glass or ceramic bowl, cover with water and soak overnight, or for at least 12 hours. Drain the rice.

Line a metal or bamboo steamer with a piece of muslin cloth. Put the rice on top of the muslin and cover the steamer with a tight-fitting lid. Put the steamer over a pot of boiling water and steam over moderately low heat for 50 minutes, or until the rice is cooked. Transfer the rice to a large bowl and fluff it up with a fork.

Toast the sesame seeds in a dry pan over medium heat for 3–4 minutes, shaking the pan gently, until the seeds are golden brown. Remove from the pan immediately to prevent them burning.

Pour the coconut milk into a small saucepan, add the sugar and 1/4 teaspoon of salt. Slowly bring the mixture to the boil, stirring constantly, until the sugar is dissolved. Lower the heat and simmer for 5 minutes, or until the mixture is slightly thickened. Stir the mixture often while it is simmering, to prevent it sticking to the bottom of the pan.

Slowly pour the coconut milk over the top of the rice. Use a fork to lift and fluff up the rice. Do not stir the liquid through, otherwise the rice will become too gluggy. Let the rice mixture rest for 20 minutes before carefully spooning it into the centre of four warmed serving bowls. Arrange the mango slices on the rice mounds. Spoon a little coconut cream over the rice, sprinkle over the sesame seeds and garnish with the mint leaves.

short-grain rice

a quick guide to short grains

Short-grain rices vary in length—some are very short and round, others have medium-to-short grains. These rices are generally higher in amylopectin. This is a starch which easily dissolves in water and creates a sticky, soft texture when cooked. It is perfect for dishes that require a sticky rice for a second cooking, as in Asian-style risotto cakes (see the recipe on page 84). It is also ideal for wetter, creamier, less fluffy dishes.

risotto rice

Risotto is perhaps the best example of the culinary potential of short-grain rice. This creamy, oozy dish is created by making grains of rice absorb a flavoured stock. If you want to make the perfect risotto, you need a rice that will perform two divergent tricks. It must partly dissolve to achieve the clinging, creamy texture that characterises risotto, but, at the same time, it should deliver firmness to the bite, or an *al dente* rice. Italians suggest the two top grades of rice for this result: *superfino* (super-fine), followed by fino. Arborio is a popular rice of the *superfino* type; others in the range include carnaroli and baldo. A good fino rice is Europa. The *semifino* (semi-fine) rice vialone nano is third in the rank and it is the choice for looser Veneto-style risottos, soups or *arancini* (rice croquettes, see page 91). It is a shorter, smaller grain than arborio and contains less amylopectin.

spanish grains

The ingredients that make up an authentic paella (Spain's national dish), everything from snails and rabbit to seafood and chicken, are the subject of much controversy. Yet there is common consent on the correct texture of the finished dish, as this is the key to quality and authenticity. In Spain, paella is not fluffy like pilaff or oozy like risotto. Instead, it is somewhere in between—slightly creamy, glistening with oil and flavour. The type of rice used is what creates the real paella feel. Valencia is the prized Spanish grain for this dish as it cooks up tender, moist and clingy due to its high starch content. Bomba, from the Spanish region of Calasparra, is another premium rice. If you can't find either of these Spanish rices, simply use arborio, pearl rice or any medium-grain rice, such as baldo, American CalRiso or Australian Calrose. These are good for risotto, too.

japanese styles

Glutinous or sticky rice is stickier still. It is perfect for sushi (see the recipe on page 121), where the grains must hold together under their mantles of fish. In the rest of Asia, outside of Japan, its most common use is in dessert. Rices labelled Chinese or Japanese sticky, pudding rice or pearl rice are good for these sweet, sticky treats.

other rice roles

Short-grain rice is wonderful by itself, but one of its most exciting roles is as a stuffing for many Mediterranean-style vegetable and seafood dishes (see the recipe for stuffed squid on page 97). The soft, absorbent grains of risotto rice are particularly good for this dish as they soak up flavours well. Summer rice salads also benefit from short-grain rices. Combining full-flavoured imaginative ingredients, rice salads can be a refreshing addition to the table. Brown short-grain rice works well, as the bran that remains on the rice serves to keep the grains separate—stickiness is the last texture you want in a rice salad.

scallops on asian risotto cakes

The zesty flavours of Asian cooking and the sea, and the tender, creamy texture of risotto are all rolled into one to make these irresistible seafood morsels. Serve them as finger food at parties or as an entree—but be warned, your main dish will have a hard act to follow.

500 ml (2 cups) vegetable stock
2 tablespoons mirin
1 stalk lemon grass (white part only), bruised
2 makrut (kaffir) lime leaves
3 fresh coriander (cilantro) roots
2 tablespoons fish sauce
1 tablespoon butter
2–3 tablespoons peanut oil
3 Asian shallots, thinly sliced
4 spring onions (scallions), chopped
3 garlic cloves, chopped
2 tablespoons finely chopped fresh ginger
1 1/4 teaspoons white pepper
140 g (2/3 cup) short-grain rice

coriander pesto
2 tablespoons toasted unsalted chopped peanuts
50 g (1 cup) chopped fresh coriander (cilantro) leaves
2 garlic cloves, chopped
1 teaspoon finely chopped fresh ginger
60 ml (1/4 cup) lime juice
1–2 teaspoons grated palm sugar

oil, for pan-frying
plain (all-purpose) flour, to dust
1 tablespoon vegetable oil, extra
16 large white scallops without roe, cleaned

Serves 4 as a starter

Heat the stock, mirin, lemon grass, lime leaves, coriander roots, half the fish sauce and 250 ml (1 cup) of water in a saucepan. Bring to the boil, then reduce to a simmer.

Heat the butter and 1 tablespoon of the peanut oil in a saucepan over medium heat until bubbling. Add the shallots, spring onion, garlic, ginger and 1 teaspoon of the white pepper. Cook for 2–3 minutes. Stir in the rice and toss until well coated.

Add 125 ml (1/2 cup) of the stock (remove the lemon grass, lime leaves and coriander roots). Stir constantly over medium heat until nearly all the liquid is absorbed. Continue adding the stock, 125 ml (1/2 cup) at a time, stirring constantly, for 25 minutes, or until the stock is absorbed and the rice is tender and creamy. Remove from the heat, cool, then cover and refrigerate for 3 hours.

To make the pesto, combine the peanuts, coriander, extra garlic and ginger, and the remaining pepper in a blender or food processor. Process until finely chopped. With the motor running, slowly add the lime juice, palm sugar and remaining fish sauce and the peanut oil and process until smooth—you might not need all the oil.

Divide the risotto into four balls, mould into patties, cover and refrigerate for 10 minutes. Heat the oil in a frying pan over medium heat. Dust the patties with flour and cook, in batches, for 2 minutes on each side. Drain on paper towels. Cover and keep warm.

Heat the extra oil in a clean frying pan over high heat. Cook the scallops for 1 minute on each side. Serve a cake with four scallops, some pesto and lime wedges, if desired.

steamed glutinous rice in lotus leaves

These are a dim sum classic that also make good savoury snacks. When steamed, the rice takes on the flavours of the other ingredients and of the lotus leaves themselves. The parcels can be made ahead and frozen, then steamed from frozen for 40 minutes.

660 g (3 cups) short-grain glutinous rice
4 large lotus leaves

filling
2 tablespoons dried shrimp
4 dried Chinese mushrooms
2 tablespoons oil
350 g (12 oz) skinless chicken breast
   fillet, cut into 1 cm (1/4 in) cubes
1 garlic clove, crushed
2 Chinese sausages (lap cheong),
   thinly sliced
2 spring onions (scallions), thinly sliced
1 tablespoon oyster sauce
3 teaspoons light soy sauce
3 teaspoons sugar
1 teaspoon roasted sesame oil
1 tablespoon cornflour
chilli sauce

Makes 8

Put the rice in a bowl, cover with cold water and leave to soak overnight. Drain in a colander and put the rice in a bamboo steamer lined with a tea towel. Steam, covered, over simmering water in a wok for 30–40 minutes, or until the rice is cooked. Cool slightly before using. Soak the leaves in boiling water for 1 hour, or until softened. Shake dry and cut the leaves in half to give eight equal pieces.

To make the filling, soak the dried shrimp in boiling water for 1 hour, then drain. Soak the dried mushrooms in boiling water for 30 minutes, then drain and squeeze out any excess water. Remove, discarding the stems, and finely chop the caps.

Heat a wok over high heat, add half the oil and heat. Stir-fry the chicken for 3 minutes. Add the dried shrimp, mushrooms, garlic, sausage and spring onion. Stir-fry for another 2 minutes. Add the oyster and soy sauces, sugar and sesame oil, and stir to combine. Mix the cornflour with 185 ml (3/4 cup) of water, stir into the sauce and simmer until thickened.

With wet hands, divide the rice into 16 balls. Put the leaves on a flat surface, put a ball of rice in the centre of each leaf and slightly flatten the ball, indenting the middle. Spoon one-eighth of the filling onto each ball, top with another flattened ball and smooth into one. Wrap by folding the leaves over to form an envelope.

Put the parcels in three steamers. Cover and steam over simmering water in a wok, for 30 minutes, reversing the steamers halfway through. Open up each leaf and eat rice from the leaf with the chilli sauce.

baked chicken
and leek risotto

60 g (2¼ oz) butter
1 leek, thinly sliced
2 chicken breast fillets, cut into small cubes
440 g (2 cups) risotto rice
60 ml (¼ cup) white wine
1¼ litres (5 cups) chicken stock
35 g (⅓ cup) grated Parmesan cheese
2 tablespoons thyme leaves
thyme leaves, to garnish
freshly grated Parmesan cheese, extra

Serves 4

Preheat the oven to 150°C (300°F/Gas 2)
and put a 5-litre (175 fl oz) ovenproof dish
with a lid in the oven. Heat the butter in a
saucepan over medium heat, stir in the
leek and cook for about 2 minutes, then
add the chicken and stir for 3 minutes.
Toss in the rice and stir for 1 minute. Add
the wine and stock, and bring to the boil.
Pour into the ovenproof dish and cover.
Cook in the oven for 30 minutes, stirring
halfway through. Remove from the oven
and stir in the cheese and thyme. Season,
then sprinkle with extra thyme and cheese.

risotto nero

2 medium-sized squid
1 litre (4 cups) fish stock
100 g (3½ oz) butter
1 red onion, finely chopped
2 garlic cloves, crushed
350 g (1⅔ cups) risotto rice
3 sachets of squid or cuttlefish ink, or the
   ink sac of a large cuttlefish
185 ml (¾ cup) white wine
2 teaspoons olive oil

Serves 6 as a starter

Cut off the heads of the squid, just below
the eyes, then cut off the tentacles.
Discard the heads and set aside the
tentacles. Thoroughly rinse the bodies,
pulling out the transparent quills, then
finely chop the bodies and set aside.

Put the fish stock in a saucepan, bring to
the boil, then maintain at a low simmer.

Heat the butter in a wide, heavy-based
saucepan and cook the onion until
softened but not browned. Increase the
heat and add the chopped squid. Cook
for 3–5 minutes, or until the squid turns
opaque. Add the garlic and stir briefly,
then add the rice and reduce the heat to
low. Season and stir briefly to coat the rice.

Squeeze out the ink from the sachets and
add to the rice with the wine. Increase the
heat and stir until all the liquid has been
absorbed. Stir in a ladleful of the stock
and cook over moderate heat, stirring
continuously. When the stock has been
absorbed, stir in another ladleful. Repeat
this process for about 20 minutes, until all
the stock has been added and the rice is
al dente. (You may not need to use all the
stock, or you may need a little extra—
every risotto will be slightly different.)

Heat the olive oil in a frying pan and fry
the tentacles quickly. Garnish the risotto
with the tentacles and serve immediately.

arancini

A speciality of Sicily, these small savoury rice balls have a golden crust which has earned them their name 'little oranges'. Saffron is used to give the base flavour and colour, while a semi-fine rice called vialone nano provides a glutinous texture to bind the mixture.

pinch of saffron threads
250 ml (1 cup) white wine
100 g (3¹/2 oz) butter
1 onion, finely chopped
1 large garlic clove, crushed
750 ml (3 cups) chicken stock
2 tablespoons thyme
220 g (1 cup) risotto rice
50 g (1³/4 oz) Parmesan cheese, grated
100 g (3¹/2 oz) fresh mozzarella or fontina
  cheese, cut into cubes
75 g (³/4 cup) dried breadcrumbs
oil for deep-frying

Makes 20

Leave the saffron to soak in the wine while you prepare the risotto. Melt the butter in a saucepan. Add the onion and garlic, and cook over low heat for 4 minutes, or until softened but not browned. Heat the stock to simmering point in another saucepan.

Add the thyme and rice to the onion. Cook, stirring, for 1 minute. Add the wine and saffron, and stir until all the wine is absorbed. Add several ladles of the hot stock, stirring continuously so that the rice cooks evenly. Keep adding enough stock to just cover the rice, stirring frequently. Repeat this process for about 20 minutes, or until the rice is creamy.

Add more water or chicken stock if the rice is not fully cooked. Make sure all the liquid is absorbed. Remove from the heat and stir in the Parmesan cheese, then spread out onto a tray covered with clingfilm. Leave to cool and, if possible, leave in the fridge overnight.

To make the arancini, roll a small amount of risotto into a walnut-sized ball. Press a hole in the middle with your thumb, put a cheese cube inside and press the risotto around it to enclose it in a ball. Repeat with the rest of the risotto. Roll each ball in the breadcrumbs, pressing down to coat well.

Heat enough oil in a deep frying pan to fully cover the arancini. Heat the oil to 180°C (350°F), or until a piece of bread fries golden brown in 15 seconds when dropped in the oil. Deep-fry the arancini in batches, without crowding the pan, for 3–4 minutes. Drain on paper towels and leave for a couple of minutes before eating. Serve hot or at room temperature.

a generous amount of parmesan cheese is essential for a good creamy risotto

asparagus risotto

asparagus risotto

1 kg (2 lb 4 oz) asparagus
1 litre (4 cups) chicken stock
4 tablespoons olive oil
1 onion, finely chopped
360 g (1²/₃ cups) risotto rice
85 g (3 oz) Parmesan cheese, grated
3 tablespoons thick (double/heavy) cream

Serves 4

Wash the asparagus and remove the woody ends (hold the spear at both ends and bend it gently—it will snap at its natural breaking point). Separate the tender tips from the stems.

Cook the asparagus stems in boiling water for about 8 minutes, or until very tender. Drain and put in a blender with the chicken stock. Blend for 1 minute, then put in a saucepan, bring to the boil and maintain at a low simmer.

Cook the asparagus tips in boiling water for 1 minute, drain and refresh in iced water.

Heat the olive oil in a wide, heavy-based saucepan. Add the onion and cook until softened but not browned. Add the rice and reduce the heat to low. Season and stir briefly to thoroughly coat the rice. Stir in a ladleful of the simmering stock and cook over moderate heat, stirring continuously. When the stock has been absorbed, stir in another ladleful. Continue this process for about 20 minutes, until all the stock has been added and the rice is *al dente*. (You may not need to use all the stock, or you may need a little extra—every risotto will be slightly different.)

Add the Parmesan cheese and cream, and gently stir in the asparagus tips. Season with salt and pepper, and serve hot.

lemon and herb risotto

1 litre (4 cups) chicken or vegetable stock
pinch saffron threads
2 tablespoons olive oil
2 leeks, thinly sliced
2 garlic cloves, crushed
360 g (1²/₃ cups) risotto rice
2–3 teaspoons finely grated lemon zest
2–3 tablespoons lemon juice
2 tablespoons chopped flat-leaf
  (Italian) parsley
2 tablespoons snipped chives
85 g (3 oz) Parmesan cheese, grated
110 g (¹/₂ cup) mascarpone cheese
1 tablespoon butter
1 tablespoon virgin olive oil
200 g (7 oz) flat mushrooms, cut into slices
1 tablespoon balsamic vinegar

Serves 4

Bring the stock and saffron to the boil, reduce the heat, cover and keep at a low simmer. Heat the olive oil in a saucepan over medium heat. Add the leek, cook for 5 minutes, then add the garlic and cook until golden. Add the rice and stir for 1 minute, or until well coated with the oil.

Add half the lemon zest and juice, stir in a ladleful of the simmering stock and cook over moderate heat, stirring continuously. When the stock has been absorbed, stir in another ladleful. Continue this process for 20 minutes, or until the rice is *al dente*. (You may not need to use all the stock, or you may need a little extra—every risotto is different). Stir in the parsley, chives, Parmesan cheese, mascarpone and the remaining zest and juice, then remove from the heat, cover and keep warm.

Melt the butter and virgin olive oil in a frying pan, add the mushrooms and balsamic vinegar and cook, stirring, over high heat for 5–7 minutes. Serve the risotto in bowls topped with the mushrooms.

stuffed squid

Originally, rice-filled meals were a way of making more expensive ingredients go further.

Some tasty creations have resulted from this imperative, like this Mediterranean-style dish.

tomato sauce
4 large ripe tomatoes
1 tablespoon olive oil
1 onion, finely chopped
1 garlic clove, crushed
60 ml (^{1}/4 cup) red wine
1 tablespoon chopped oregano

stuffing
1 tablespoon olive oil
2 spring onions (scallions), chopped
280 g (1^1/2 cups) cold, cooked risotto rice
60 g (2 oz) pine nuts
75 g (2^1/2 oz) currants
2 tablespoons chopped flat-leaf
  (Italian) parsley
2 teaspoons finely grated lemon zest
1 egg, lightly beaten

1 kg (2 lb 4 oz) medium squid hoods

Serves 4

Preheat the oven to 160°C (315°F/Gas 2–3). For the tomato sauce, score a cross in the base of each tomato, soak them in a bowl of boiling water for about 10 seconds, then plunge them into cold water. Peel the skin from the cross and chop the flesh. Heat the oil in a frying pan. Add the onion and garlic, and cook over low heat for about 2 minutes, stirring frequently, until the onion is soft. Add the tomato, wine and oregano, and bring to the boil. Reduce the heat, cover and cook over low heat for 10 minutes.

Meanwhile, for the stuffing, mix all the ingredients except the egg in a bowl. Add enough egg to moisten the ingredients.

Wash the squid and pat dry with paper towels. Spoon the stuffing into each hood until three-quarters full and secure the ends with toothpicks or skewers. Put the stuffed squid in a single layer in a casserole dish.

Pour the tomato sauce over the squid, cover the dish and bake for 20 minutes, or until the squid are tender. Cut the squid into thick slices. Spoon the tomato sauce over the squid just before serving.

NOTE: You will need to cook about 110 g (^{1}/2 cup) of short-grain rice for this recipe. The cooking time for the squid will depend on its size. Always choose small squid because it is more tender.

california rolls

Maki-sushi is the name given to this popular rice snack rolled in dried seaweed. Sliced, it offers an aesthetically pleasing appetizer, and the different textures of the ingredients in the roll make it particularly delicious. Simply put, it's sheer pleasure on a platter.

220 g (1 cup) sushi rice
1 tablespoon rice vinegar
2 generous pinches of caster
    (superfine) sugar
1 large egg
1 teaspoon sake
1 teaspoon oil
2 sheets roasted nori seaweed, each
    measuring 20 x 18 cm (8 x 7 in)
2 crabsticks, 40 g each (1^{1}/2 oz each),
    cut into strips
25 g (1 oz) pickled daikon, cut into
    matchsticks
25 g (1 oz) carrot, cut into matchsticks
25 g (1 oz) cucumber, cut into
    matchsticks
Japanese soy sauce
wasabi paste
pickled ginger

Serves 4

Rinse the rice under cold running water. Put the rice into a saucepan and cover with 200 ml (7 fl oz) cold water. Cover the pan and bring the water to the boil. Reduce the heat and simmer for 10 minutes.

While the rice is cooking, mix together the vinegar, a pinch of the sugar and a pinch of salt. When the rice is cooked, remove the pan from the heat and leave, covered, for 10 minutes. Transfer the rice to a bowl. Add the vinegar mixture, bit by bit, turning and folding the rice using a wooden spoon. Continue to fold until the rice is cool. Cover the pan with a damp tea towel and set aside—do not refrigerate.

To make the omelette, gently combine the egg, sake, the remaining pinch of sugar and a pinch of salt. Heat the oil in a small square or round frying pan. Add the egg mixture and cook until firm around the edges but still slightly soft in the middle. Roll the omelette, then tip it out of the pan. Cool, then slice into strips.

Put a nori sheet on the mat, shiny-side-down. Add half of the rice, leaving a 2 cm (1 in) gap at the edge furthest away from you. Lay half of the fillings on the rice in the following order: omelette; crabstick; daikon; carrot; cucumber. Starting with the end nearest to you, tightly roll the mat and the nori. Repeat this process with the remaining ingredients.

Using a sharp knife, cut each roll into six slices. After cutting each slice, rinse the knife under cold running water to prevent sticking. Transfer the sliced sushi to a serving plate and serve with soy sauce, wasabi and pickled ginger.

milanese risotto

185 ml (³/4 cup) dry white vermouth
   or white wine
large pinch of saffron threads
1.5 litres (6 cups) chicken stock
100 g (3¹/2 oz) butter
85 g (3 oz) beef marrow
1 large onion, finely chopped
1 garlic clove, crushed
330 g (1¹/2 cups) risotto rice
55 g (2 oz) Parmesan cheese, grated

Serves 6 as a side dish

Put the white vermouth in a bowl, add the
saffron and leave to soak. Put the chicken
stock in a saucepan, bring to the boil,
then maintain at a low simmer.

Melt the butter and beef marrow in a
large, wide, heavy-based saucepan. Add
the onion and garlic, and cook until
softened but not browned. Add the rice
and reduce the heat to low. Season with
salt and pepper, and stir briefly to
thoroughly coat the rice.

Add the vermouth and saffron to the rice.
Increase the heat and cook, stirring, until
all the liquid has been absorbed. Stir in a
ladleful of the simmering stock and cook
over moderate heat, stirring continuously.
When the stock has been absorbed, stir in
another ladleful. Continue this process for
about 20 minutes, until all the stock has
been added and the rice is *al dente*. (You
may not need to use all the stock, or
you may need a little extra—every risotto
will be slightly different.)

Stir in a handful of the grated Parmesan
cheese and serve the rest on the side for
everyone to help themselves.

risi e bisi

1.5 litres (6 cups) chicken or vegetable
   stock
2 teaspoons olive oil
40 g (1³/4 oz) butter
1 onion, finely chopped
85 g (3 oz) pancetta, cut into small cubes
2 tablespoons chopped parsley
375 g (13 oz) shelled young peas
220 g (1 cup) risotto rice
50 g (1³/4 oz) Parmesan cheese, grated

Serves 4

Put the stock in a saucepan, bring to the
boil, then maintain at a low simmer. Heat
the oil and half the butter in a wide,
heavy-based saucepan. Cook the onion
and pancetta over low heat for 5 minutes,
or until softened. Stir in the parsley and
peas, then add 2 ladlefuls of the stock.
Simmer for 6–8 minutes.

Add the rice and the remaining stock.
Simmer until the rice is *al dente* and most
of the stock has been absorbed. Stir in the
remaining butter and the Parmesan cheese,
season with salt and pepper, and serve.

minestrone alla milanese

225 g (8 oz) dried borlotti beans
55 g (2 oz) butter
1 onion, finely chopped
1 garlic clove, finely chopped
3 tablespoons parsley, finely chopped
2 sage leaves
100 g (3^1/$_2$ oz) pancetta, cubed
2 celery stalks, halved, then sliced
2 carrots, sliced
3 potatoes, peeled but left whole
1 teaspoon tomato paste (purée)
400 g (14 oz) tin chopped tomatoes
8 basil leaves
3 litres (12 cups) chicken or vegetable stock
2 zucchini (courgettes), sliced
225 g (8 oz) shelled peas
125 g (4^1/$_2$ oz) runner beans, cut into
　4 cm (1^1/$_2$ in) lengths
^{1}/$_4$ cabbage, shredded
220 g (1 cup) risotto rice
grated Parmesan cheese, to serve

Serves 6

Put the dried beans in a large bowl, cover with cold water and soak overnight. Drain and rinse under cold water.

Melt the butter in a saucepan and add the onion, garlic, parsley, sage and pancetta. Cook over low heat, stirring once or twice, for 10 minutes, or until the onion is soft.

Add the celery, carrot and potatoes, and cook for 5 minutes. Stir in the tomato paste, tomatoes, basil and borlotti beans. Season with pepper. Add the stock and bring slowly to the boil. Cover and leave to simmer for 2 hours, stirring once or twice.

If the potatoes have not broken up, roughly break them with a fork against the side of the pan. Taste for seasoning and add the zucchini, peas, runner beans, cabbage and rice. Simmer until the rice is cooked. Serve with the Parmesan cheese.

garlic and thyme are a great flavour fusion for rich risottos

red wine risotto

red wine risotto

500 ml (2 cups) chicken stock
100 g (3 1/2 oz) butter
1 onion, finely chopped
1 large garlic clove, crushed
2 tablespoons chopped thyme
220 g (1 cup) risotto rice
500 ml (2 cups) dry red wine
50 g (1 3/4 oz) Parmesan cheese, grated

Serves 4 as a starter

Put the chicken stock in a saucepan, bring to the boil, then maintain at a low simmer.

Heat the butter in a wide, heavy-based saucepan. Add the onion and garlic, and cook until softened but not browned. Add the thyme and rice, and reduce the heat to low. Season and stir briefly to thoroughly coat the rice.

Add half the red wine. Increase the heat and cook, stirring, until all the liquid has been absorbed. Stir in a ladleful of the simmering stock and cook over moderate heat, stirring continuously. When the stock has been absorbed, stir in another ladleful. Continue like this for 10 minutes, until you have added half the stock.

Add the remaining red wine to the risotto, stirring continuously until it has been absorbed. Stir in another ladleful of the stock, then continue for 10 minutes, until all the stock has been added and the rice is *al dente*. (You may not need to use all the stock, or you may need a little extra— every risotto will be slightly different.)

Stir in half the grated Parmesan cheese just before serving with the remaining cheese to be sprinkled on top.

mushroom risotto

15 g (1/2 oz) packet dried porcini mushrooms
1 litre (4 cups) vegetable or chicken stock
2 tablespoons olive oil
1 tablespoon butter
1 small onion, finely chopped
2 garlic cloves, crushed
385 g (1 3/4 cups) risotto rice
250 g (9 oz) fresh mushrooms, sliced
pinch nutmeg
45 g (1 3/4 oz) Parmesan cheese, grated
3 tablespoons finely chopped parsley

Serves 4

Soak the porcini in 500 ml (2 cups) boiling water for 30 minutes. Drain, retaining the liquid. Chop the porcini mushrooms and pass the liquid through a fine sieve. Put the stock in a saucepan, bring to the boil, then maintain at a low simmer.

Heat the olive oil and butter in a wide, heavy-based saucepan. Cook the onion and garlic until softened but not browned, then add the rice and reduce the heat to low. Season and stir briefly to thoroughly coat the rice. Toss in the fresh mushrooms and nutmeg. Season with salt and black pepper, and cook, stirring, for 2 minutes. Add the porcini mushrooms, and their liquid, increase the heat and cook until all the liquid has been absorbed.

Stir in a ladleful of stock and cook over moderate heat, stirring continuously. When the stock has been absorbed, stir in another ladleful. Continue like this for about 20 minutes, until all the stock has been added and the rice is *al dente*. (You may not need to use all the stock, or you may need a little extra.) Remove from the heat and stir in the Parmesan cheese and parsley. Season and serve.

seafood risotto

It may seem like the classic comfort dish for winter, but you can indulge in risotto all year-round, just by varying the ingredients. In the warmer months, make the most of seasonal seafood and sun-loving tomatoes, and celebrate the fresh flavours of summer.

2 ripe tomatoes
500 g (1 lb 2 oz) black mussels
315 ml (1¼ cups) white wine
1.25 litres (5 cups) fish stock
pinch saffron threads
2 tablespoons olive oil
30 g (1 oz) butter
500 g (1 lb 2 oz) raw prawns (shrimp),
    peeled and deveined
225 g (8 oz) squid tubes, sliced into
    thin rings
200 g (7 oz) scallops
3 garlic cloves, crushed
1 onion, finely chopped
440 g (2 cups) risotto rice
2 tablespoons chopped parsley

Serves 4

Score a cross in the base of each tomato. Put in a bowl of boiling water for about 10 seconds, then plunge into cold water and peel away the skin from the cross. Chop the tomato flesh.

Scrub the mussels with a stiff brush and remove the beards. Discard any broken mussels or those that do not close when tapped. Pour the wine into a large saucepan and bring to the boil. Add the mussels and cook, covered, over medium heat for 3–5 minutes, or until the mussels open. Discard any that do not open. Strain, reserving the liquid. Remove the mussels from their shells.

Combine the reserved mussel liquid, stock and saffron in a large saucepan, cover and keep at a low simmer.

In a separate large saucepan, heat the olive oil and butter over medium heat. Add the prawns and cook until pink. Remove. Add the squid and scallops, and cook for about 1–2 minutes, until white. Remove. Add the garlic and onion, and cook for 3 minutes, or until golden. Add the rice and stir until coated.

Add 125 ml (½ cup) of the simmering liquid, stirring constantly, until all of it is absorbed. Continue adding the hot liquid, 125 ml (½ cup) at a time, stirring constantly for 25 minutes, or until all the liquid is absorbed. Stir in the tomato, seafood and parsley, and heat through. Season with salt and pepper, and serve.

japanese rice balls

275 g (1¹/4 cups) sushi rice
330 ml (1¹/3 cups) water
2 teaspoons black sesame seeds
55 g (2 oz) smoked salmon, chopped
2 tablespoons finely chopped
  pickled ginger
2 spring onions (scallions), finely chopped

Serves 4

Wash the rice thoroughly in a sieve under cold running water until the water runs clear. Put the rice in a heavy-based saucepan with the water and bring to the boil. Reduce the heat to very low, cover and cook for 15 minutes. Remove the pan from the heat and stand, covered, for about 20 minutes.

Dry-roast the sesame seeds in a frying pan over low heat, constantly shaking the pan, for about 1–2 minutes, or until the sesame seeds begin to pop.

Combine the smoked salmon, ginger and spring onion in a small bowl. Using wet hands, form a small handful of rice into a ball, push 2 teaspoons of the smoked salmon mixture into the centre of the rice and remould the ball around it. Repeat with the remaining rice and salmon, keeping your hands wet to prevent the rice from becoming sticky.

Arrange the balls on a serving platter and sprinkle with the sesame seeds.

risotto cakes with lemon mayonnaise

For fusion food at its delectable best, try these zesty little numbers. The combination of rich, sun-ripened condiments from the Mediterranean, creamy savoury rice and mayonnaise speckled with a Middle Eastern relish packs a powerful flavour punch.

1 litre (35 fl oz) chicken stock
1 tablespoon olive oil
1 garlic clove, finely chopped
1 small onion, finely chopped
220 g (1 cup) risotto rice
125 ml ($1/2$ cup) dry white wine
4 marinated artichokes, drained and
  finely chopped
25 g ($1/4$ cup) coarsely grated Parmesan
  cheese
1 teaspoon grated lemon zest
60 g ($1/2$ cup) plain (all-purpose) flour
2 eggs, beaten
100 g (1 cup) dry breadcrumbs
3 slices (50 g or $13/4$ oz) of pancetta
oil, for pan-frying
15 pitted Kalamata olives, halved
flat-leaf (Italian) parsley, to garnish

lemon mayonnaise
80 g ($1/3$ cup) whole-egg mayonnaise
2 teaspoons finely chopped
  preserved lemon

Makes 30 cakes

Pour the stock into a saucepan and bring to the boil. Reduce the heat, cover with a lid and keep at a low simmer.

Heat the oil in a large saucepan and cook the garlic and onion over low heat for 5 minutes, or until the onion has softened. Stir in the rice for 1 minute, or until it is coated in the oil. Pour in the wine and stir over medium heat until all the wine is absorbed. Add 125 ml ($1/2$ cup) of the simmering stock, and stir constantly, until most of the stock is absorbed. Pour in more stock, 125 ml ($1/2$ cup) at a time, stirring constantly, until it is completely absorbed, then add another 125 ml ($1/2$ cup). Repeat this process for 20 minutes until the rice is tender and the mixture creamy. Stir in the artichokes, Parmesan cheese and zest.

Spread the risotto on a tray and allow to cool for 2 hours. Put the flour, egg and breadcrumbs in three separate bowls. Using wet hands, roll the risotto into 30 x 3 cm (1 in) wide x 1.5 cm ($1/2$ in) high discs. Coat the rice discs with flour, dip them in the egg, then coat in the breadcrumbs. Refrigerate for at least 30 minutes.

Cook the pancetta in a non-stick frying pan until crisp. Tear each slice into 10 pieces.

To make the mayonnaise, mix the preserved lemon into the mayonnaise.

Heat the oil in a frying pan and cook the risotto cakes in batches for 2–3 minutes on each side, or until golden and crisp. Drain on crumpled paper towels. Top each cake with $1/2$ teaspoon of the mayonnaise, a piece of pancetta, half an olive and a torn parsley leaf. Serve warm or hot.

chicken domburi

Japanese comfort food is perfect for those cold winter days—a steaming bowl of rice topped with tasty chicken and egg. It's a one-dish meal, so its virtues are simplicity and good flavour. The word *domburi* is the name of the earthenware in which the dish is served.

440 g (2 cups) sushi or short-grain rice
2 tablespoons oil
200 g (7 oz) chicken breast fillet, cut into thin strips
2 onions, thinly sliced
4 tablespoons Japanese soy sauce
2 tablespoons mirin
1 teaspoon dashi granules
5 eggs, lightly beaten
2 sheets nori
2 spring onions (scallions), sliced

Serves 4

Wash the rice in a colander under cold running water until the water runs clear. Put the rice in a medium, heavy-based saucepan, add 625 ml (2 1/2 cups) of water and bring to the boil over high heat. Cover the pan with a tight-fitting lid, reduce the heat to the lowest setting to prevent the rice burning at the bottom of the pan and cook for 15 minutes. Turn the heat to very high for 15–20 seconds and remove the pan from the heat. Set the pan aside for 12 minutes, without lifting the lid (so the steam does not escape).

Heat the oil in a frying pan over high heat, stir-fry the chicken until it is golden and tender, and set aside. Reheat the pan, add the onion and cook, stirring occasionally, for 3 minutes or until it begins to soften. Add 2 tablespoons of water, soy sauce, mirin and dashi granules. Stir to dissolve the dashi and bring the stock to the boil. Cook for 3 minutes, until the onion is tender.

Return the chicken to the pan and pour in the eggs, stirring gently to break up the eggs. Cover and simmer over very low heat for 2 to 3 minutes or until the eggs are just set. Remove the pan from the heat.

Toast the nori by holding it over low heat and moving it back and forth for about 15 seconds, then crumble it into a dish.

Transfer the rice to an earthenware dish, carefully spoon over the prepared chicken and egg mixture, and sprinkle over the nori. Garnish with the spring onion.

the subtle taste of french shallots is perfect for delicately-flavoured seafood risottos

scallop, fennel and chilli risotto

scallop, fennel and chilli risotto

1.25 litres (5 cups) chicken stock
250 ml (1 cup) dry white wine
1 tablespoon olive oil
55 g (2 oz) butter
3 French shallots, finely sliced
1 baby fennel bulb, finely chopped, and
    2 tablespoons green tops, to garnish
2 garlic cloves, crushed
3 anchovy fillets preserved in oil, drained
1/2 teaspoon fennel seeds, crushed
1/2 teaspoon dried chilli flakes
330 g (1 1/2 cups) risotto rice
600 g (1 lb 5 oz) medium fresh scallops,
    roe and shell removed
2 tablespoons chopped flat-leaf
    (Italian) parsley
1 tablespoon snipped chives

Serves 4

Put the stock and wine in a saucepan and bring to the boil over high heat. Reduce the heat to low and keep at a low simmer.

Heat the oil and half the butter in a separate saucepan over medium heat, add the shallots and fennel, and cook for 5 minutes. Add the garlic, anchovies, fennel seeds and dried chilli, and stir for 1 minute.

Add the rice and stir for 1 minute. Add a ladleful of the simmering stock and cook over moderate heat, stirring continuously. When the stock is absorbed, stir in another ladleful. Repeat this process for 20 minutes, until all the stock has been added and the rice is *al dente*. (You may not use all the stock, or you may need a little extra—every risotto will be different.) Add the scallops in the last 5 minutes and continue to stir.

When the scallops have turned white and are cooked through, stir in the parsley and remaining butter. Season. Garnish with 2 tablespoons of finely chopped fennel tops and the chives, then serve immediately.

grilled rice with dipping sauce

2 eggs
1 tablespoon fish sauce
1/2 teaspoon sugar
660 g (3 cups) cooked glutinous
    short-grain rice, well drained

dipping sauce
125 ml (1/2 cup) white rice vinegar
115 g (4 oz) sugar
2 garlic cloves, crushed
2 birds eye chillies, finely chopped

Makes 6 skewers

Preheat the grill (broiler) to its highest heat setting.

To make the dipping sauce, combine all the ingredients in a small bowl and stir until the sugar is dissolved.

Beat the eggs with the fish sauce, sugar and a pinch of black pepper.

Divide the cooked rice into six portions and form each one into three small balls. Press each ball to flatten. Thread three flat rounds onto each skewer.

Line a grill tray with foil and brush it lightly with oil. Dip each rice skewer into the egg mixture, shake off any excess and put it on the grill tray. Grill the rice until it is browned on one side, then turn it over and grill the other side. You can also cook these on a barbecue (grill), if you like.

Serve the skewers with the dipping sauce while they are still very hot.

chirashi sushi

If you enjoy the taste of sushi but haven't mastered the Japanese art of shaping rice, try your hand at 'scattered' or *chirashi* sushi. In this recipe, the ingredients are casually mixed together. It's an easy make-ahead appetizer or main course served at room temperature.

4 dried shiitake mushrooms
440 g (2 cups) sushi rice
4 tablespoons rice vinegar
4 tablespoons caster (superfine) sugar
1 tablespoon soy sauce
2 large eggs
1 tablespoon sake
1–2 teaspoons oil
1 avocado
1 tablespoon lemon juice
1 small carrot, peeled, cut
   into thin strips and blanched
300 g (10 1/2 oz) salmon fillet, skinned and
   cut into small chunks
2 spring onions (scallions), trimmed and
   finely shredded
2 tablespoons crushed roasted white
   sesame seeds or 50 g (1 3/4 oz) fish roe
sliced pickled ginger
wasabi
Japanese soy sauce

Serves 4

Put the mushrooms in a bowl and cover with 300 ml (10 1/2 fl oz) of boiling water. Set aside. Rinse the rice, put in a saucepan, and cover with 500 ml (2 cups) of cold water. Bring to the boil, reduce the heat and simmer for about 10 minutes.

Combine the rice vinegar, 2 tablespoons of the sugar and 2 teaspoons of salt. When the rice is cooked, remove the pan from the heat and leave, covered, for 10 minutes.

Transfer the rice to a mixing bowl. Add the rice vinegar mixture, bit by bit, turning and folding the rice with a wooden spoon. Continue to fold until the rice is cool. Cover the pan with a damp tea towel and leave to one side; do not refrigerate.

Add the remaining 2 tablespoons of sugar and the soy sauce to the mushrooms, bring the liquid to the boil, then simmer, covered, for 15 minutes. Drain.

Beat the eggs with the sake and a pinch of salt. Heat the oil in a small frying pan or Japanese omelette pan, add half of the egg mixture and cook until just set. Roll the omelette to one side of the pan. Pour in the remaining egg and lift the cooked omelette so the raw egg runs underneath it. When the second omelette is cooked, roll the two together, and allow to cool. Cut into thin slices.

Thinly slice the mushrooms, discarding the stalks. Cut the avocado into cubes and toss in the lemon juice. Arrange the mushrooms, omelette, carrot, avocado, salmon and spring onions on the rice. Scatter with the sesame seeds or roe and serve with ginger, wasabi and soy sauce.

chickpeas with rice

2 tablespoons olive oil
1 onion, finely chopped
1 garlic clove, crushed
1 red chilli, finely chopped
1 litre (4 cups) chicken stock
4 ripe tomatoes, peeled, seeded
  and diced
1 cinnamon stick
1 bay leaf
220 g (1 cup) short- or medium-grain rice
400 g (14 oz) tin chickpeas, drained
2 tablespoons chopped parsley
2 tablespoons chopped mint
olive oil
feta cheese

Serves 4

Heat the olive oil in a large saucepan and
add the onion, garlic and chilli. Fry, stirring
frequently, until all the ingredients are soft
and the onion is translucent.

Add the stock, tomatoes, cinnamon, bay
leaf and rice, and bring to the boil. Reduce
the heat to low and simmer for 15 minutes,
or until the rice is almost tender.

Stir in the chickpeas and cook for another
2–3 minutes, then stir in the parsley and
mint, and season well.

Serve in soup bowls drizzled with olive oil
and topped with crumbled feta cheese.

japanese-style brown rice salad

220 g (1 cup) short-grain brown rice
2 tablespoons oil
1 garlic clove, thinly sliced
4 spring onions (scallions), finely sliced
2 tablespoons pickled ginger, finely sliced
1/2 daikon, grated
1 tablespoon mirin
2 teaspoons sesame oil
2 tablespoons toasted sesame seeds
2 fillet steaks
2 tablespoons teriyaki sauce

Serves 4

Cook the rice in boiling water until tender
but firm, about 40 minutes. Drain and cool.
Heat 1 tablespoon of oil in a frying pan
and cook the garlic and spring onion until
fragrant, then add to the rice with the
ginger and daikon. Sprinkle on the mirin,
and sesame oil and seeds. Toss together.

Brush the steak fillets with teriyaki sauce
and fry in the remaining oil for 3 minutes
on each side. Rest for 1 minute, slice thinly
and add a few strips to the rice salad.

123

sushi hand-rolls

Roll-your-own sushi is a great way to entertain. Just lay out the ingredients and let everyone be their own host. The trick is to have plenty of rice on hand and a good supply of sake, beer or tea to keep the ball rolling. Start by showing your guests how it's done.

220 g (1 cup) sushi rice
2 tablespoons rice vinegar
generous pinch caster (superfine) sugar
175 g (6 oz) sashimi grade fish, such as
  tuna or salmon
6 sheets roasted nori seaweed, each
  measuring 20 x 18 cm (8 x 7 in)
1 small avocado
1 tablespoon lemon juice
wasabi paste
60 g (2¼ oz) pickled daikon
85 g (3 oz) cucumber, cut into thin strips
Japanese soy sauce
pickled ginger

Serves 6

Rinse the rice under cold running water. Put the rice into a saucepan and cover with 200 ml (7 fl oz) cold water. Cover the pan and bring the water to the boil, then reduce the heat and simmer for 10 minutes.

Mix together 1 tablespoon of the vinegar, the sugar and ¼ teaspoon of salt. When the rice is cooked, remove it from the heat and let it stand, covered, for 10 minutes. Transfer the rice to a mixing bowl. Add the rice vinegar mixture, bit by bit, turning and folding the rice with a wooden spoon. Continue to fold until the rice is cool. Cover with a damp tea towel and set aside, do not refrigerate.

Meanwhile, using a sharp knife, cut the fish into 16 paper-thin pieces, measuring 2 x 5 cm (¾ x 2 in). Cut each sheet of seaweed in half. Thinly slice the avocado and sprinkle with a little lemon juice. Mix the remaining tablespoon of vinegar with 3 tablespoons of water in a small bowl. Use the vinegar water to stop the rice sticking to your fingers as you form the sushi. Taking 1 tablespoon of rice at a time, carefully mould the rice into oval shapes—you should end up with 12 ovals.

Holding a piece of nori seaweed in the palm of your hand, smear a little wasabi over it, put an oval of rice on top, then fill it with a piece of fish, avocado, daikon and cucumber. Wrap the seaweed around the ingredients in a cone shape, using a couple of grains of cooked rice to secure the rolls. Alternatively, put the ingredients on the table for guests to help themselves. Serve the sushi with soy sauce, extra wasabi and pickled ginger.

vine-ripened tomatoes give paella a fresh flavour boost

chicken paella

chicken paella

60 ml (1/4 cup) olive oil
1 large red capsicum (pepper), seeded
  and cut into 5 mm (1/4 in) strips
600 g (1 lb 5 oz) chicken thigh fillets, cut
  into 3 cm (11/4 in) cubes
200 g (7 oz) chorizo, cut into
  2 cm (3/4 inch) slices
200 g (7 oz) mushrooms, thinly sliced
3 garlic cloves, crushed
1 tablespoon grated lemon zest
700 g (1 lb 9 oz) ripe tomatoes,
  roughly chopped
200 g (61/2 oz) green beans, cut into
  3 cm (11/4 inch) lengths
1 tablespoon chopped rosemary
2 tablespoons chopped flat-leaf
  (Italian) parsley
1/4 teaspoon saffron threads dissolved
  in 60 ml (1/4 cup) hot water
440 g (2 cups) paella or medium-grain rice
750 ml (3 cups) hot chicken stock
6 lemon wedges, to serve

Serves 6

Heat the olive oil in a paella pan, or in a
heavy-based deep frying pan over medium
heat. Add the capsicum and cook, stirring,
for 6 minutes. Remove from the pan. Toss
in the chicken and cook for 10 minutes,
until brown on all sides. Remove from the
pan. Add the chorizo to the pan and cook
for 5 minutes. Remove from the pan. Add
the mushrooms, garlic and lemon zest
to the pan, and cook over medium heat
for about 5 minutes.

Stir in the tomato and capsicum, and cook
for another 5 minutes, or until the tomato
is soft. Add the beans, rosemary, parsley,
saffron mixture, rice, chicken and sausage.
Stir briefly and add the stock. Do not stir
at this point. Reduce the heat and simmer
for 30 minutes. Remove from the heat,
cover and leave to stand for 10 minutes.
Serve with lemon wedges.

seafood paella

125 ml (1/2 cup) white wine
1 red onion, chopped
12–16 black mussels, cleaned
125 ml (1/2 cup) olive oil
1/2 red onion, extra, finely chopped
1 rasher bacon, finely chopped
4 garlic cloves, crushed
1 red capsicum (pepper), finely chopped
1 ripe tomato, peeled and chopped
90 g (31/4 oz) chorizo, thinly sliced
pinch cayenne pepper
220 g (1 cup) paella or medium-grain rice
1/4 teaspoon saffron threads
500 ml (2 cups) chicken stock, heated
115 g (4 oz) white fish fillets, skinned and
  cut into pieces
85 g (3 oz) fresh or frozen peas
12 raw prawns (shrimp), peeled and
  deveined
2 squid tubes, cleaned and cut into rings
2 tablespoons finely chopped parsley

Serves 4

Heat the wine and onion in a saucepan.
Add the mussels, cover and gently shake
the pan for 5 minutes over high heat.
Remove from the heat, discard any closed
mussels and drain, reserving the liquid.
Heat the oil in a frying pan, add the extra
onion, bacon, garlic and capsicum, and
cook for 5 minutes. Add the tomato,
chorizo and cayenne. Season. Stir in the
reserved liquid, then add the rice and stir.

Blend the saffron with the stock, add to
the rice and mix well. Bring to the boil,
reduce the heat to low and simmer,
uncovered, for 15 minutes without stirring.

Put the peas and seafood on top of the
rice. Push them in, cover and cook over
low heat for 10 minutes, or until the rice
is tender and the seafood is cooked. Add
the mussels for the last 5 minutes. If the
rice is not quite cooked, add extra stock
and cook for a few more minutes. Leave
for 5 minutes, then add parsley and serve.

baked rice pudding

55 g (^{1}/4 cup) pudding, short- or
   medium-grain rice
410 ml (1^2/3 cups) milk
1^1/2 tablespoons caster (superfine) sugar
185 ml (^{3}/4 cup) cream
^{1}/4 teaspoon natural vanilla extract
^{1}/4 teaspoon grated nutmeg
1 bay leaf (optional)

Serves 4

Preheat the oven to 150°C (300°F/Gas 2)
and grease four 250 ml (1 cup) ramekins.
In a bowl, mix together the rice, milk,
caster sugar, cream and vanilla essence,
and pour into the greased dish. Dust the
surface with the grated nutmeg and float
the bay leaf on top for a little extra
flavour, if you wish.

Bake the rice puddings for about 1 hour,
until the rice has absorbed most of the
milk, the texture is creamy and a brown
skin has formed on top. Serve hot.

venetian rice pudding

750 ml (2^1/2 cups) milk
250 ml (1 cup) thick (double/heavy) cream
1 vanilla pod, split
50 g (1^3/4 oz) caster (superfine) sugar
^{1}/4 teaspoon ground cinnamon
pinch grated nutmeg
1 tablespoon grated orange zest
85 g (3 oz) sultanas
2 tablespoons brandy or sweet Marsala
110 g (^{1}/2 cup) risotto or pudding rice

Serves 4

Put the milk, double cream and vanilla
pod in a heavy-based saucepan, and bring
just to the boil, then remove from the
heat. Add the sugar, cinnamon, nutmeg
and orange zest, and set aside.

Put the sultanas and brandy in a small bowl
and leave to soak. Add the rice to the
infused milk and return to the heat. Bring
to a simmer and stir slowly for 35 minutes,
or until the rice is creamy. Stir in the
sultanas and remove the vanilla pod at the
end of cooking. Serve warm or cold.

rice ice cream

A rice confection can make for a sweet ending to a meal. The rice in this dessert provides a surprising crunchy effect in the cool and creamy gelato, and the candied citron adds a tangy fruit note. Serve this popular Italian ice cream with a fruit sauce or fresh berries.

110 g (1/2 cup) risotto rice
750 ml (3 cups) milk
1 vanilla bean
3 tablespoons sugar
500 ml (2 cups) thick
   (double/heavy) cream
3 teaspoons icing (confectioners') sugar

custard
125 ml (1/2 cup) milk
3 egg yolks
6 tablespoons sugar
2 tablespoons finely chopped
   candied citron

Serves 4

Put the rice in a saucepan, add the milk, vanilla bean, sugar and a pinch of salt. Bring to a boil over medium heat, stirring constantly. Reduce the heat to low and simmer for about 12 minutes. Remove the rice from the heat and set aside for about 2 hours to cool completely.

Pour the contents of the pan through a colander and drain away the excess liquid. Let the rice stand for 30 minutes.

To make the custard, heat the milk in a saucepan over medium heat until it is almost boiling. In a bowl, whisk together the egg yolks and sugar, and add the milk. Mix well. Rinse the pan and return the milk mixture to the pan. Cook, stirring constantly, over a low heat until the custard thickens and will easily coat the back of a wooden spoon. Remove the custard from the heat and allow to cool.

Transfer the rice to a bowl, remove the vanilla bean, add the custard and mix well. Add the cream, icing sugar and candied citron, and stir well to combine.

Pour the mixture into a freezer box and freeze for 1 hour. Take the box out of the freezer and give the mixture a good stir, then refreeze. Repeat this process four times until the mixture is almost solid. The more you stir, the less icy the mixture.

Alternatively, you can freeze the mixture in an ice-cream machine, following the manufacturer's instructions.

Remove the ice cream from the freezer 10 minutes before serving to soften. If it is too frozen the rice grains will be very hard.

coloured rice

a quick guide to coloured rice

Some speciality rices are prized not for their aroma, but for their brilliant colour. This category of rice covers all grains that are not white (or brown) after the husk has been removed. Inside the husk is the outer bran coating, comprising three layers—the pericarp is the layer containing the colouring, either red, black or purple. The long, slender grain of wild rice, the seed of a North American aquatic grass, is tawny blond to almost black.

red selection

Red rice has a red bran layer and covers a spectrum from short- to medium-grain rices to long grains. Camargue red rice is a medium-grain *japonica* grown as a small crop in France. This high-quality grain is expensive and not so readily available, but you may find it in speciality European food stores. Its colour and texture make it perfect for a summer rice salad (see the recipe on page 141). A less expensive alternative is Bhutanese red rice. This is a coloured *japonica* from central Asia and is tender, absorbent, but slightly sticky, so it is easy to eat with chopsticks. Thai red rice (grown among jasmine rice) has similar qualities, as does Vietnamese red cargo. If you are using either of these coloured rices in a salad, give them a rinse after cooking so the grains don't stick together.

Wehani is a russet-coloured rice derived from basmati. It looks much like Thai red rice, though its grains are bigger. The chewiness of this rice lends itself to reheating, so if you have leftovers, add it to soups or stews. Its fresh grainy taste stands up to robust-flavoured dishes.

black coats

Black rice is actually a white rice coated in a black-coloured bran. There are myriad varieties, from Chinese black rice, suitable for congee, to black sticky rice, otherwise known as Thai black rice or Balinese black and purple rice. The Indonesian varieties are great carriers of flavour and cook up to a beautiful shiny indigo colour. Their unique plate presentation makes them a must for added eye appeal. They are typically used in desserts (see the recipe for black rice pudding on page 150).

the wild bunch

Hundreds of years ago, in the big lakeland district between Canada and the United States, it would be a familiar sight to find two American-Indian women harvesting wild rice in a canoe. Traditional harvesting still goes on today, but largely wild rice is cultivated and harvested mechanically.

Natural wild rice can be expensive, so it is often extended with brown or white rice—this also gives it added texture, colour and taste. Compared to rice, this grass seed is richer in protein and other nutrients, and has a distinctive smoky, nutty flavour. It is particularly good as a stuffing for fish and poultry.

cooking notes

Because coloured rice is unmilled, like brown rice, it can take 40–60 minutes to cook, depending on whether you prefer a tender or more chewy texture. Soaking the rice overnight in cold water reduces the cooking time. The rice can then be boiled for 20–30 minutes. Coloured rices are also good when mixed with white rice (see the recipe for stuffed chicken on page 138). If mixing coloured and white rice, cook them separately, then combine them.

chicken with wild rice and nut stuffing

For a fresh take on roast stuffed chicken, try adding wild rice. Its nutty flavour complements the macadamia and pistachio nuts used in the filling, while the sweet, tangy taste of the cranberries and orange juice provides a wonderful foil to the rice.

65 g (^{1}/3 cup) wild rice
200 g (1 cup) basmati rice
60 ml (^{1}/4 cup) orange juice
100 g (3^1/2 oz) dried cranberries
^{1}/2 teaspoon ground cinnamon
100 g (3^1/2 oz) macadamia nuts, roasted
   and roughly chopped
55 g (2 oz) shelled pistachio nuts
2 teaspoons chopped fresh rosemary
zest of 1 large orange
1 tablespoon melted butter
1.6–2 kg (3 lb 8 oz–4 lb 4 oz) chicken
1 large onion
1 carrot
2 celery stalks
1 tablespoon plain (all-purpose) flour

Serves 4

Add the wild rice to a saucepan of cold, salted water. Bring to the boil, simmer for 10 minutes, then add the basmati rice and cook for 15 minutes. While the rice is cooking, bring the orange juice to the boil in a small saucepan and add the dried cranberries. Remove from the heat and leave to soak for 15 minutes.

Drain the rice under cold water, then cool. Transfer to a bowl, add the cranberries, cinnamon, macadamias and pistachio, rosemary and zest. Season well. Stir the butter through the mixture, then cool.

Preheat the oven to 200°C (400°F/Gas 6). Pat dry the inside of the chicken with paper towels. Fill the cavity with the prepared cold stuffing, taking care not to pack it too tightly, as stuffing expands during cooking. Tuck the wings under the chicken and tie the legs securely with string. Any excess skin at the neck of the

bird can be tucked under the wings. Spread the remaining butter over the skin of the chicken, then season well with sea salt and pepper. Put the chicken, breast-side-up, on a roasting rack (see below), then prepare the vegetables.

Chop the vegetables into large chunks. Spread out the vegetables in a roasting tin. Put the chicken, on its rack, over the vegetables and roast for 45 minutes. Remove from the oven, tilt the tin slightly and scoop up the juices to baste the chicken. Return to the oven for another 30 minutes, or until the chicken is tender and the juices run clear when the thigh is pierced with a skewer. If the chicken is not cooked, return it to the oven for another 10–15 minutes. Cover loosely with foil if it is browning too quickly.

When the chicken is cooked, transfer it to a serving dish, cover and allow to rest while you prepare the gravy.

Remove the vegetables from the roasting tin with a slotted spoon and discard. Spoon out all but 3 tablespoons of the fat from the roasting tin, then put the tin on the stovetop. Stir in the flour and cook for 1 minute, until it starts to brown. Scrape the crusty bits from the base. Add the remaining stock and cook for 3–4 minutes. Add any chicken juices from the serving dish. Strain the gravy through a sieve and keep it warm. For a very glossy gravy, whisk 15 g (^{1}/2 oz) of cold butter into the gravy just before straining.

red-rice salad

Camargue red rice from France is a superior grain, so it's more expensive than other varieties. The USA and Asia also grow red rice—you can use either type for this scrumptious salad. Just remember to drain it well as it retains more water than other grains.

220 g (1 cup) Camargue red rice
4 tablespoons olive oil
1 red capsicum (pepper)
1 yellow capsicum (pepper)
1 red onion, cut into slivers
2 zucchini (courgettes), diced
1 tablespoon butter
1 garlic clove, crushed
1 chicken breast with skin on
2 tablespoons lemon juice
2 tablespoons chopped basil
2 tablespoons chopped parsley

Serves 4

Put the red rice in a saucepan with plenty of boiling water and cook for 30 minutes or until tender. Drain well, then cool.

Preheat the grill (broiler) to hot. Brush the red and yellow capsicum with some of the olive oil and grill on all sides until the skin is blistered and black. Leave to cool briefly, then peel off the skin and cut the capsicum into strips. Add the capsicum strips to the rice.

Fry the onion and zucchini in more of the oil until lightly charred around the edges. Add the onion and zucchini to the rice.

Mix the butter with the garlic. Push the mixture under the skin of the chicken breast so it is evenly distributed. Grill the chicken on both sides until the skin is crisp and the breast is cooked through. Leave the chicken to rest for 2 minutes, then slice it into strips (you can discard the skin, if you like). Add the chicken slices to the rice with any juices.

Add the lemon juice, any remaining olive oil and the herbs, and toss together. Season well and serve immediately.

baked sea bass with wild rice stuffing

2 small fennel bulbs
65 g (1/3 cup) wild rice
250 ml (1 cup) fish stock
2 tablespoons butter
2 tablespoons olive oil
1 onion, chopped
1 garlic clove, crushed
grated zest of 1 lemon
2 kg (4 lb 8 oz) sea bass, bass or any large
  white fish, gutted and scaled
extra virgin olive oil
1 lemon, quartered
2 teaspoons chopped oregano
lemon wedges, to serve

Serves 4

Preheat the oven to 190°C (375°F/Gas 5)
and lightly grease a large, shallow
ovenproof dish. Finely slice the fennel,
reserving the green fronds.

Put the wild rice and stock in a saucepan
with 3 tablespoons of water and bring to
the boil. Simmer for 30 minutes, or until
tender, then drain. Heat the butter and
olive oil in a large frying pan and gently
cook the fennel, onion and garlic for
12–15 minutes, or until softened but not
browned. Add the lemon zest, stir in the
rice and season with salt and pepper.

Put the fish on a chopping board. Stuff the
fish with a heaped tablespoon of the fennel
mixture and a quarter of the reserved
fennel fronds. Transfer to an ovenproof
dish. Brush with extra virgin olive oil,
squeeze over the lemon and season well.

Spoon the remainder of the cooked fennel
into the ovenproof dish and sprinkle
with half the oregano. Put the fish on top of
the fennel. Sprinkle the remaining oregano
over the fish and loosely cover the dish with
foil. Bake for 25 minutes, or until it is just
cooked through. Serve with lemon wedges.

pecans add to the nutty taste of wild rice

duck with wild rice

duck with wild rice

dressing
80 ml (¹/3 cup) oil
2 teaspoons walnut oil
1 teaspoon grated orange zest
2 tablespoons orange juice
1 tablespoon chopped preserved ginger

95 g (¹/2 cup) wild rice
2 teaspoons oil
50 g (1³/4 oz) pecans, roughly chopped
¹/2 teaspoon ground cinnamon
65 g (¹/3 cup) long-grain rice
2 tablespoons finely chopped parsley
4 spring onions (scallions), thinly sliced
2 duck breasts
zest of 1 orange

Serves 4

To make the dressing, thoroughly mix the ingredients together. Season with salt and black pepper. Set aside.

Put the wild rice in a saucepan with 300 ml (10 fl oz) water. Bring to the boil, then cook, covered, for 30 minutes, or until tender. Drain away any excess water. Meanwhile, heat the oil in a large frying pan. Add the pecans and cook, stirring, until golden. Add the cinnamon and a pinch of salt, and cook for 1 minute.

Cook the rice in a saucepan of boiling water until tender. Drain and mix with the wild rice and pecans in a large, shallow bowl. Add the parsley and spring onion. Add half the dressing and toss well.

Put the duck, skin-side-down, in a cold frying pan, then heat the pan over a high heat. Cook for 5 minutes until crisp, then turn over and cook for another 5 minutes. Tip out any excess fat and add the remaining dressing and the orange zest, and cook until bubbling. Transfer the duck to a serving dish and slice diagonally. Serve with the rice, drizzled with any juices.

quail stuffed with wild rice

50 g (¹/4 cup) wild rice
250 ml (1 cup) chicken stock
1 onion, finely chopped
1 tablespoon butter
1 tablespoon finely chopped
  dried apricots
1 tablespoon finely chopped prunes
1 tablespoon chopped mixed parsley
  and chervil
4 quail
4 tablespoons olive oil

Serves 4

Heat the oven to 200°C (400°F/Gas 6). Put the wild rice and chicken stock in a saucepan and bring to the boil. Simmer for 30 minutes, or until tender, then drain.

Sauté the onion in the butter for 5 minutes. Then add the apricots, prunes, parsley and chervil. Add the rice and season well.

Loosely fill the quails with the prepared rice stuffing and fasten them closed with cocktail sticks.

Heat the oil in a frying pan and brown the quails all over. Transfer to a roasting tin and cook for 15–20 minutes or until a skewer inserted into the cavity comes out very hot. Serve the quails with a green salad and potatoes.

wild rice soup

95 g (¹/2 cup) wild rice
1 tablespoon oil
1 onion, finely chopped
2 celery stalks, finely chopped
1 green capsicum (pepper), finely
  chopped
4 rashers bacon, rind removed and
  finely chopped
4 open cap mushrooms, finely sliced
1 litre (4 cups) chicken stock
125 ml (¹/2 cup) cream
1 tablespoon finely chopped parsley

Serves 6

Put the wild rice in a saucepan with plenty
of water and bring to the boil. Cook for
40 minutes or until the rice is tender. Drain.

Heat the oil in a large saucepan and add
the onion, celery, capsicum and bacon.
Fry until the onion is soft and the bacon
browned. Add the mushroom and cook
for 1–2 minutes. Add the chicken stock
and bring to the boil, add the rice, then
stir and cook the mixture for 2 minutes.
Remove the pan from the heat.

Stir in the cream and parsley, then reheat
until the soup is almost boiling. Serve in
deep bowls with bread.

wild rice salad

95 g (¹/2 cup) wild rice
250 ml (1 cup) chicken stock
1 tablespoon butter
100 g (¹/2 cup) basmati rice
2 rashers bacon, rind removed, chopped
  and cooked
110 g (³/4 cup) currants
60 g (¹/2 cup) slivered almonds, toasted
30 g (1 cup) chopped parsley
6 spring onions (scallions), finely sliced
grated zest and juice of 1 lemon
olive oil, to drizzle
lemon wedges, to serve

Serves 4

Put the wild rice and stock in a saucepan,
add the butter, bring to the boil, then
cook, covered, over low heat for 1 hour.
Drain. Put the basmati rice in a separate
saucepan with cold water and bring to the
boil. Cook at a simmer for 12 minutes,
then drain. Mix with the wild rice and cool.
Combine the rice with the bacon, currants,
almonds, parsley, spring onions and lemon
zest and juice. Season, drizzle with olive
oil and serve with lemon wedges.

sticky black rice pudding

Black rice is grown in Thailand, Indonesia and the Philippines and is actually a dark garnet red. It's the core of many Asian desserts and in this wicked treat the rice is scented and sweetened with pandanus leaves. Serve with fresh tropical fruit to offset the richness.

400 g (2 cups) black sticky rice
3 fresh pandanus leaves
500 ml (2 cups) coconut milk
85 g (3 oz) palm sugar, grated
3 tablespoons caster (superfine) sugar
coconut cream, to serve
mango or papaya cubes, to serve

Serves 6

Put the rice in a large glass or ceramic bowl and cover with water. Leave to soak for at least 8 hours, or overnight. Drain, then put in a saucepan with 1 litre (4 cups) of water and slowly bring to the boil. Cook at a slow boil, stirring frequently, for 20 minutes, or until tender. Drain.

Shred the pandanus leaves with your fingers, then tie them in a knot. Pour the coconut milk in a large saucepan and heat until almost boiling. Add the palm sugar, caster sugar and pandanus leaves, and stir until the sugar is dissolved.

Add the rice to the pan and cook, stirring, for about 8 minutes without boiling. Remove from the heat, cover and leave for 15 minutes to absorb the flavours. Remove the pandanus leaves.

Spoon the rice into individual bowls and serve warm with coconut cream and fresh mango or papaya cubes.

glossary

al dente Meaning 'to the tooth'. Pasta and risotto rice are cooked until they are *al dente*—the outside is tender but the centre still has a little resistance or 'bite'.

arroz Spanish and Portuguese for rice.

asafoetida (hing) This yellowish powder is made from the dried latex of a type of fennel. Its pungent smell has earned it the name 'devil's dung'. It is said to be one of the secret ingredients of Worcestershire sauce. Asafoetida is used as a meat tenderizer and is also added to pulses to make them more digestible. It comes in small airtight containers and is available from Indian food shops.

chinese mushrooms The Chinese usually cook with dried mushrooms, which have a strong flavour and aroma, and need to be soaked to reconstitute them before they are used. The flavourful soaking liquid can be added to dishes. Dried mushrooms are widely available.

chorizo A highly seasoned ground pork sausage flavoured with garlic, chilli powder and other spices. It is widely used in both Mexican and Spanish cooking. Mexican chorizo is made with fresh pork, while the Spanish version uses smoked pork.

clams Also sold as vongole, these bivalves are slightly chewy and salty, and have a hard, ridged shell, measuring about 4 cm (1½ in). They are often confused with pipi, which have a smooth (sometimes larger) shell, and a sweeter meat.

dal or dhal is used to describe not only an ingredient but also a dish made from it. In India, dal relates to any type of dried split pea, bean or lentil. All dal should be rinsed before use, and cooking times vary.

ghee A highly clarified butter made from cow or water buffalo milk. Ghee can be heated to a high temperature without burning and has an aromatic flavour.

ginger (adrak) The rhizome of a tropical plant which is sometimes referred to as a 'root'. Fresh young ginger has a smooth, pinkish beige skin. As it ages, the skin toughens and the flesh becomes more fibrous. Choose pieces you can snap easily.

harissa A fiery red paste from North Africa, made of chilli which is soaked, then pounded with coriander, caraway, garlic and salt, and moistened with olive oil.

ikan bilis The fry of anchovies, similar to whitebait, which are salted and sundried. Ikan bilis is used in Southeast Asian dishes and is available in Asian food stores.

lemon grass A lemon-scented tropical grass (*Cymbopogon citratus*) with leaves and a central rib. It is popular in Southeast Asia, mostly because lemons do not grow so easily in the tropics. Only the lower stalk is used in cooking. You can substitute one stalk for three thin strips of lemon zest.

makrut (kaffir) lime leaves The highly fragrant, dark green leaves of the *Citrus hystrix* tree, which are available fresh, frozen or dried from greengrocers.

mirin Sometimes incorrectly described as 'rice wine', this spirit-based sweetener from Japan is used for cooking, especially in marinades and glazes, and simmered dishes. It is sold in Asian food shops.

nori A seaweed which is pressed into sheets and dried. It is mostly used as a wrapper in sushi or is shredded and added to Japanese soups as a garnish.

one-thousand-year-old eggs
Also known as century eggs, these are eggs that have been preserved by coating them in wood ash, slaked lime and rice husks. They are left to mature for 40 days. When ready to eat, the coating is scraped off and the shell peeled. These eggs are eaten as an hors d'oeuvre or with congee.

pandanus leaf Also known as pandan leaf, this flavour enhancer is used in both savoury and sweet dishes of Sri Lanka, Malaysia, Indonesia and Thailand. It has a delicate, almost sweet taste. A strip may be added to rice on cooking or to simmering curries. It is also used to wrap ingredients, such as chicken and rice.

passata Meaning 'puréed', this most commonly refers to a smooth uncooked tomato pulp bought in tins or jars.

pickled daikon A yellow-coloured, firm and crunchy pickle made from daikon—a large white radish. It is usually pickled in dry rice bran after being hung to dry. It is available as whole pieces or presliced in supermarkets or Asian food stores.

pickled ginger Whole, sliced or shredded peeled ginger root preserved in brine, rice wine or rice vinegar. It usually takes on a light pink colouring through chemical reaction. Thinly sliced pink ginger pickled in sweet vinegar is frequently used as a garnish in Japanese dishes.

preserved lemons Lemons that have been preserved in a salt–lemon juice mixture (sometimes with spices such as cinnamon, cloves and coriander) for about 30 days. They are an indispensable ingredient in Moroccan cooking. Rinse and remove the white pith before using.

saffron The dried dark orange stigmas of a type of crocus flower, which are used to add aroma and flavour to food. Only a few threads are needed for each recipe as they are very pungent (and expensive).

sake is a Japanese alcoholic drink which is often called rice wine—a misnomer since it is brewed. It is often served warm in restaurants, but is also used as an ingredient to tenderize, tone down saltiness and to remove unwanted flavours and scents. Sake is stronger than mirin, so it should be used sparingly.

salt cod Brought to Europe from Newfoundland as long ago as the fifteenth century, salt cod's popularity in France is a legacy of the religious requirement to eat fish on Fridays. Salt cod has been gutted, salted and dried, and is different from stockfish, which is dried but not salted. A centre-cut fillet tends to be meatier than the thinner tail end, and some varieties are drier than others so soaking time varies. Salt cod is also sold as *morue* or *bacalao*.

sashimi Thinly sliced raw fish, typically served with grated horseradish or ginger and soy sauce. The preparation of the fish is a skill perfected with long practice.

shaoxing rice wine Made from rice, millet, yeast and Shaoxing's local water, this is aged for at least three years, then bottled either in glass or decorative earthenware bottles. Several varieties are available. As a drink, rice wine is served warm in small cups. In cooking, dry sherry is the best substitute.

turmeric (haldi) Dried turmeric, sold whole or ground, is a deep yellow colour, and has a slightly bitter flavour and pungent aroma. Turmeric is added to dishes for both colour and flavour.

wasabi paste A pungent Japanese flavouring resembling horseradish in taste. It comes from the herb *Wasabia japonica* and is turned into a green powder (which is reconstituted with water) or wasabi paste, both available from Asian food stores.

zest The outer layer of citrus fruit, which is coloured and contains the essential oils.

153

index

Published by Murdoch Books®, a division of Murdoch Magazines Pty Ltd.

Murdoch Books® Australia
GPO Box 1203
Sydney NSW 1045
Phone: + 61 (0) 2 4352 7000
Fax: + 61 (0) 2 4352 7026

Murdoch Books UK Limited
Ferry House
51–57 Lacy Road
Putney, London SW15 1PR
Phone: + 44 (0) 20 8355 1480
Fax: + 44 (0) 20 8355 1499

Creative Director, Designer: Marylouise Brammer
Editorial Director: Diana Hill
Editor: Raffaela Pugliese
Production: Janis Barbi
Food Director: Lulu Grimes
Photographer: Ian Hofstetter
Stylist: Katy Holder
Food Preparation: Ross Dobson

Recipes developed and written by Sophie Braimbridge, Belinda Frost, Jo Glynn, Deh-Ta Hsiung, Sarah Randell, Nina Simonds and the Murdoch Books Test Kitchen.

Chief Executive: Juliet Rogers
Publisher: Kay Scarlett

National Library of Australia Cataloguing-in-Publication Data
Rice: from risotto to rice pudding.
Includes index. ISBN 1 74045 146 5.
1. Cookery (Rice).
641.6318

The publisher thanks the following for their assistance: AEG Kitchen Appliances; Breville Holdings Pty Ltd; Chief Australia; Kitchen AID; The Bay Tree; ici et la; Malcolm Greenwood; MUD Australia; No Chintz.

IMPORTANT: Those who might be at risk from the effects of salmonella food poisoning (the elderly, pregnant women, young children and those suffering from immune deficiency diseases) should consult their GP with any concerns about eating raw eggs.